GET MINTED!

Learn to Grow Massive Wealth in the Midst of Uncertainties

BY NORA A. GAY

Get Minted!

ISBN: 978-1087899213

Category: BUSINESS & ECONOMICS/Personal Finance/Life Insurance

Author's note

In mid-March 2020, Covid-19 forced people around the world to reconsider their way of life seriously. Ordered to self-quarantine, those with a stake in the financial markets went into a frenzy. Even those who had professional advice through financial or investment advisors felt unprepared and unsettled by the market volatility. Our approach to personal finance as a society has been too narrow; we make singular decisions that are unable to withstand the test of uncertain times.

Life presents many challenges. Similarly, the road to wealth can offer many detours. These stories illustrate just that. While I often use humor to keep you engaged with my storytelling abilities, you will quickly realize how seriously I take the matter. My seriousness, however, must not surprise you considering the cover of this book. Be honest: you believe I look like the wife of a dictator. I will not share the identity of the person who so eloquently described my cover image thus, and I have changed the names of the people in my stories to protect their privacy.

While the book is not in any particular timeline, you will most likely discern an inevitable progression in the severity of the stories. For a good laugh, I might exaggerate reactions. If you are not up for a giggle while discussing what, for some, is possibly the most boring subject on the planet, feel free to take the essence. As my mom says, these stories are likely only funny to me and those involved.

TABLE OF
CONTENTS

PREFACE

Warning! Get Minted! is not your typical personal finance book. It is a journey through discovery and independence. And that is how you Get Minted! We all tread down different paths in life. We go where our families, our jobs, our education, and our personal preferences lead us. Somewhere down at the end of all these winding trails is that one perfect destination we all seek: financial freedom.

 The freedom to spend any amount of money when we want, on what we want, for the people we want. The freedom to not be chained to a desk or a computer nine hours a day, five days a week for the rest of our natural lives. It is a destination that many seek, but few ever reach. Why do you ask?

For starters, the road to financial freedom has several detours.

The key to reaching that final destination is to have a roadmap that prepares us for all of the possibilities to come and a strategy that accounts for all the curve balls that life will throw at us.

I realize a myriad of books has been written on the subject, offering either a motivational or a mathematical approach to achieving financial independence. You can pick up any book on the shelf, scroll through any blog post online, or click on any video channel from YouTube and be told that the way to financial freedom is to diversify your portfolio in the financial market. Most of these so-called experts fail to grasp, and seldom share, that diversification outside of the market is the real key to achieving that economic freedom and keeping yourself from suffering a mental breakdown in financial climates similar to the current one.

As you go through this book, you are going to break down some barriers that are holding you back, you are going to laugh (I hope), and you're going to gain a new understanding of what it takes to amass serious wealth successfully.

You will also gain a lot of insight via my personal experience as an advisor, which will offer you a holistic view of how to achieve your goal in an efficient, intelligent manner.

It won't surprise me if this is not the first financial advice book you have ever read. Or the fifth or even the twentieth! Struggling to be independently wealthy is one of the biggest battles we face as humans, right up there with finding the best way to lose weight and mary-kondoing our closets.

Many authors have developed systems to help you pay off your debt, dished out general rules of thumb for smart investments, refined mathematical formulas that will arm you with knowledge on when to sell and when to buy stock, and created templates to help you plan your budget wisely. Some of these are absolute essentials to assisting people to get control of their financials.

But all of them are missing one key ingredient: they do not capture the fact that life is full of changes from your birth to your death. They often do not account for the situations that will arise that will make you want to throw all of that practical advice out the window.

Like many people, I reflect on my accomplishments when the end of the year rolls around. What have I done to make my life better? What have I done to get closer to my goals? To do better for my family? To improve my career? It can be a very unpleasant process at times, but I see it as an opportunity to be truly transparent with oneself and gain some real perspective. After all,

Growth is only achievable when you are willing to take stock of yourself and see both the good and the bad.

It was about two years ago that I realized that my life was headed in the wrong direction. The worst part was that it was not obvious to the naked eye.

It was not that I did not have a good job or people who cared about me or money in the bank. I realized that while I was educating many families, my reach was minimal. That is when I started getting serious about writing this book.

I am not a professionally trained writer, but I was determined to take this beautiful journey. I want to help you get from where you are right now regarding achieving your financial freedom to where I know you can get. It is not going to be comfortable, and it is not going to be fair. Life will continue to take shots at you from all directions.

It reminds me of being on one of those crazy inner-tube rides at a water park. You get in at the top, and the only thing you can be sure of is that eventually, you're going to reach the bottom. But how you get there is anyone's guess. Sometimes you will be spun in circles after circles. Sometimes you will be traveling so fast the inner tube will end up gliding along the walls of the slide. Sometimes you will think it is the most fun you have ever had, and other times you will close your eyes and pray for it to be over soon.

Before we begin, remember one thing about yourself that nobody can take away from you: you are a mighty being, believe it! Be resilient and do not give in to fear. Work hard and get the benefits that are certain to come your way.

INTRODUCTION

"What would you do with one million dollars?" the charming disembodied voice would whisper to passersby. After stopping short in her track, the surprised millennial would see a visual of beautiful mansions, women, and yachts, and supercars. It is 2018, and Monaco seems a bit out of reach even as she strolls the streets unbothered like everyone else. The city is vibrant, and everyone seems to have no care in the world while going from boutique to boutique. Finally, it looks like even the oldest of the rushing crowds would appear as if they would stay young forever. Everyone seemed to agree that this is what retirement should look like.

At the time, I was a twenty-eight-year-old woman who, after failing to keep my founding position at a market research firm, started a wealth management practice at a small holistic financial planning firm. Our specialty was helping people plan offensively and defensively. We capitalized on protection planning to create solid business plans that would shift as our clients' economic value would change.

When it was clear that my money transfer agency built on the blockchain technology would be too costly, I had a big idea: why not offer a different kind of value to the individuals who were already paying attention?

I had no idea where I would start with that. Serendipitously, I met with the gentleman who would soon after that become my mentor in my mission to educate three hundred families within my first year in the financial advising business.

 My objective was to equip as many people as possible with the knowledge and tools necessary to live and retire well.

My mission was clear in front of me, and I was convinced I was going to revolutionize the way advisors reach and obtain new clients. I was sure I had learned how to break the training mold, which was reinforced when I attained the Platinum level of production within less than three months at my new firm. This accomplishment had never been done before by any new advisors, and I received some nice accolades from my CEO, colleagues, friends, and a spot to speak at our quarterly town hall.

I was competing for the #1 producer spot against a woman who had been in the business for nearly a decade and knew her craft like the palm of her hand. Though there was no comparison, I was sure my time had come. I was a young Black woman disrupting the financial services industry! I was to wealth management what Tesla was to electric car makers. Boy, was I wrong?

This process was so not about me. It was about those I served. Seeking recognition for the work I did became a juvenile and outright savage game I played with myself. I became nothing more than a woman with a lot of knowledge and the ability to make an absurd amount of money. This illumination left me feeling broke and dejected. I was making great money and having fun along the way. I was no doubt helping others. But, somewhere on that path, I had lost the essence of my goal. The night before the eureka moment, I was to fly to the Dominican Republic from Boston. I spent most of the night tossing and turning, thinking about whom I had become, and how desperate I was to please my superiors and leave a mark in this company for all other female and black advisors who would come after me.

I began what Jay Samit called "self-disrupting." I analyzed all the pieces that had led me to this point and how I was spending my energy. I thought of how I presented the information to potential clients and what would set me apart from other advisors. If I were going to find my way back to the mission, I would have to change something in my approach. And I asked myself, "what is the most effective and efficient way to achieve my desired goal?" After all, we all have one hundred and forty-eight hours in a week, and my goal was less than realistic when working alone.

If I were going to my desired crowd, I had to find a conduit, a platform, oh, I know, a book!

Thus, this book is my conduit to help reshape and expand your financial house.

"The big money is not in buying or selling, but in the waiting." (– Charlie Munger)

We are living in uniquely tumultuous times right now. The country is preparing for a coronavirus-fueled recession, race wars are consuming the country, pitting person against person, education is morphing into entirely digital teaching, and you're being told, especially as a millennial, that there's never going to be a piece of the financial pie left for you.

The question is: do you believe people when they tell you that, or do you believe the American Dream is still alive and well? Millennials see the American Dream differently today. They don't see it as mere financial freedom, but rather, the ability to live the life they want to live. In one survey published in the New York Times, Abrams (2019), writes that 85% of respondents indicated the American Dream meant "the freedom of choice in how to live." This new take on the American Dream transcends political parties, with 41% of survey respondents indicating their family is already living this version of the American Dream.

Contrary to what the news might try to tell you today, only 18% of those survey respondents indicated the American Dream is dead. That's right; less than one-fourth of people believe the American Dream is gone or out of reach. These are people who already have real-world experience; firsthand, that personal independence to live the life you want to live is still abundant in this country – even despite a pandemic-fueled recession.

Therefore, as we embark on this wealth journey together, I need you to drop the possibly already-ingrained victim mentality that so many have. As a millennial myself, I am not preaching at you as some Baby Boomer from greener pastures. Instead, I know the challenges our generation has had to face, but I am still asking you to rise above it and shed the excuses that 10 prevent you from genuinely growing wealth. The idea that "wealth" and "richness" in our country is evil is something you need to erase from your consciousness.

If these are some of the excuses you make daily:

- How can I ever save money? I can barely afford to make my rent.
- I'll never be able to have the job of my dreams because my debt is too big. I can't leave the job I have now, I'm locked in.
- We'll never get to benefit from social security and other financial cushions that our grandparents had.

- The American Dream is dead because of Baby Boomers. There is nothing left for millennials.
- I am too anxious to build wealth for myself. I don't know how to do it.

Then this book is for you. I want you to know you can grow sustainable, and generational wealth starting today. Anyone can do it, no matter where you come from, what you look like, or what you earn. Wealth knows no boundaries or prejudice. It's an abundance awaiting the person that dares to reach for it. For anything worth having, there will always be those fears, those risks, and those dangers to make it happen. So many millennials have grown complacent, merely accepting the status quo for fear of financial failure. I need you to let that kind of pessimism go today. With this book, I will go over everything you need to do to start building wealth for yourself. As an advisor myself, I have used these tried and true methods to grow my economic value. I didn't allow excuses to stop me from making it happen, and I don't want you to permit that, either. Imagine this: you have pure financial freedom today. How you choose to approach that concept is entirely up to you. My role is to give you the tools and resources necessary to get there. Your prerogative is to follow through. Without further ado, let's Get Minted!

CHAPTER 01

YOUR WEALTH IN THE WORLD:
BANKING AND FINANCIAL SYSTEMS

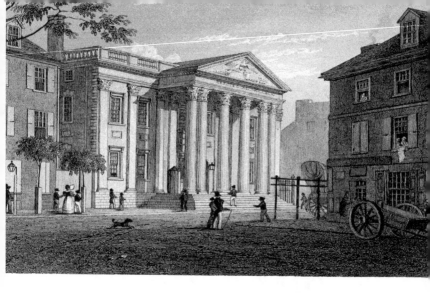

How do the financial systems that you operate inside of work? How do you make money, and whence do you determine where and when to spend it? If you were a guest in a roomful of fifth graders, could you explain these questions to them? How about if you were doing it to a lecture hall filled with college students pursuing financial degrees? Could you answer them if you were talking to yourself in the mirror?

One of the biggest misbeliefs we live with when it comes to managing our financial situations is understanding how money works. We say we know how to save money, make our money work, make enough to live by and avoid wasting it. For most people, that's a bald-faced lie.

The only systems we know are those we saw being practiced around us by parents, siblings, friends, and extended family members. If your parents struggled to make ends meet the entire time you were growing up, what do you know about doing better? If your older sister is continuously charging up her credit cards then barely getting by paying them off, what makes you think you will not do the same thing once you are a legal adult? In so many areas of our lives, we copy what we see. If we grew up in a houseful of love and kindness, we are infinitely more likely to be that way as spouses and parents. If we grew up in a home where arguments were settled by physical abuse and alcoholism, there's a lot higher probability that we will succumb to one or the other, no matter how much we despised them as children.

To truly understand how financial systems operate, we need to build our knowledge base from the ground up. You would not assume you could create a log cabin without knowing how to cut down a tree, and you should not expect you can achieve financial independence without knowing how the system works.

So let's start together at the beginning. I want you to meet your new best friend for the remainder of this book. Her name is Daisy, and she is a millennial who has gotten out of school, started her career, and suddenly found herself feeling extraordinarily trapped and limited by her financial situation.

The visions she had when she was growing up of being an independent woman with her career, her place, and the ability to explore the world, have fun, and make a name for herself are not the reality she is facing. How did she get here? And how does she get out?

Let us check in on Daisy as our story begins. She's 25; she has been out of college for three years after earning a degree in marketing. She had to take out some major-league loans for college, but she figured it was worth it to get the big-time education and start earning money with her degree. She knows that she needs to start paying the money back sooner rather than later, but she decided a flashy convertible was the perfect reward for landing her first job. Daisy has since gone on three different girls' trips with her pals from school and has also invested in a lovely townhome close to her career, the park, and nightlife spots she enjoys.

She keeps up with her bills, or at least she hasn't had to pay any late fees yet. She uses her credit card to eat, though,and when she wants something before payday.

She feels like she is running the show, but is she? She cannot make any big purchases until her paycheck comes because she's not putting anything away in savings. She is paying big chunks of interest on her car loan and her credit cards, which means those purchases keep costing her money repeatedly.

Meanwhile, her student loan payments sit idly because, under federal law, she does not have to start paying on them for a while. That doesn't mean they are accumulating more interest though. She sees the statements every month and rolls her eyes, telling herself she will soon get on it.

Daisy thinks she knows how her financial situation works. She could not be farther from the truth! She is being controlled by forces that she does not understand and trapped in a vicious cycle of accumulating debt, making interest payments on items she already purchased, and being a slave to her paycheck - she has no other means of income from which to draw funds when she wants to buy something. If she had a need, or more likely a want, between paychecks, she charges it, putting herself more in debt and adding more principal that she has to pay interest on down the road.

Daisy is suffering from consumer debt, which is the worst kind of obligation to have. She believes she will work her way out of it, but her bad spending habits are precisely what makes credit-card companies and other financial institutions so productive. Credit card companies lure consumers into believing they are keeping up with their finances by requiring them to only pay a minimum amount of their total due each month. The truth is that only paying that minimum keeps consumers in an indenture-servant type relationship with the credit card company.

Every month that your balance is not paid off in full or is only paid off in these small increments, the card's high interest rate is charged on the remaining principal, and the amount owed balloons up higher.

Only in the fine print on another page of the statement does the credit-card company show the difference in what happens if you pay only the minimum amount each month instead of more substantial amounts.

That is the spot where account holders realized that only paying the minimum means owing money for years instead of months; or for decades instead of years. When you factor in that people keep spending money on their cards until they no longer have available credit, it's easy to see how people never get out of credit card debt over the course of a lifetime.

The exact same thing happens when people take out loans for homes or automobiles. They are given a number from the lending bank on how much money they qualify for based on their current income and debt ratios. The lending banks do not care about your ability to keep living to your current standard or have enough to buy groceries and clothes and pay the light bill each month. They also would prefer you not pay off big chunks of your principal at once, because doing so reduces the amount of interest they can charge over the long haul.

Because we are so conditioned to paying the amount shown on the bill - as we do for our electricity bill or to pay for our smartphone data plan - we end up doing the same for our credit cards and loans, even though paying the minimum amount is detrimental to establishing financial independence. Daisy has had no formal training in the personal finance or in creating revenue streams beyond her regular 9-to-5 job. If she continues on this course, no matter how much money she makes, she will find it virtually impossible to get out of debt and begin building wealth. As her salary increases over time, she will use it to buy more and more things she wants in the present instead of changing her attitude to focus on driving down her debt and finding ways to invest and save her money to begin building wealth. Her blindspots will keep her from understanding that despite her college education, excellent job, pretty car, and cute apartment, she is completely controlled by financial institutions designed to bleed every cent out of her that they can for as long as they can. If something catastrophic were to happen, like say a global pandemic that saw her laid off as her company cut back to save itself, she would not have enough money saved up to pay her bills for more than the current month.

When people cannot make payments on their credit cards and other loans, their credit scores drop.

When their credit scores drop, the only way they can get loans or new credit cards is by agreeing to take them on at even higher interest rates. Their desperation for things they want in the short term cripples their ability to keep their heads above water in the long run. Even as they start to make more money over time, as most people do in the course of a career, they're spending it on paying down their increased debt.

Daisy's story is hardly an uncommon one among millennials in today's America. She fits in with a majority of the US population in two key areas: She is not living on less than she makes and is not planning to save for significant expenses. According to financial guru Chris Hogan, 94% of millionaires live on less than their means and 95% do not buy something until they can afford it. Most Americans see credit cards as a means to buy what they want, even though they cannot afford it. They also view banks merely as places to keep their money until they want to spend more of it.

This capricious spending and lack of sensible investing are two of the most significant barriers to building wealth - a term interchangeable with gaining financial freedom as you will encounter.

Before we go too far, allow me to give you a crash course into the American banking system. Unfortunately, this complex system tends to confuse all who come across it.

Although it is frustrating, it is extremely important to understand so that you can have a better idea of what is going on with your money, as stated above.

There are several different types of banking institutions that all work in almost exactly the same way. Before we get into exactly what the banks' function is in the United States, let us go over the different types of banks that exist. Keep in mind that the lines aren't drawn with permanent markers here; some banks might offer a variety of services spanning across the different types of banks listed.

Retail banks

Retail banks are the ones you come across most often. These banks focus on the consumer and provide the public with a place to deposit money into their own checkings and savings accounts. These kinds of banks give credit cards, offer loans, and offer numerous locations for you to manage your finances.

Commercial Banks

A commercial bank provides services such as accepting deposits, providing business loans, and offering basic investment products. These banks started out with the aim to serve the business sector and not just the general public. These banks rely on lines of credit to manage cash flow and provide any other kind of service a business might need.

Credit Unions

A credit union is a member-owned financial cooperative, controlled by its members to provide credit at competitive rates. In essence, a credit union is a not-for-profit organization owned by its own customers and offers banking services to its members. Although similar to commercial or retail banks, credit unions differ in that the members share common characteristics like the location of where they live, what occupation they have, and where they work.

Savings Banks

Savings banks provide a place for people to save their money and accrue interest on their money over time

Online Banks

Online banks operate entirely online and do not offer physical brick and mortar locations for you to manage your finances at. These are becoming more popular as our world becomes more digitized.

Mutual Unions

Mutual banks are similar to credit unions in that they are owned by the members or customers instead of outside investors.

Central Banks

The central bank is responsible for managing the monetary system of the government. The Federal Reserve (central bank) is responsible for managing economic activity and supervising banks. You will understand how they do this when you learn how banks function in the next section!

Banks in the US make money off of the deposit you have made in your bank account. Imagine that your dollars get pooled and lent out to other people to finance homes, cars, their business or child's education.

Before you freak out about your money getting "taken from you, I want to clarify something. Banks putting your money into this large pool for other people to use does not mean that your money disappears from your control. You can take out the money that has been credited to your account in cash whenever you want. In fact, you can take out as much as you want whenever you want, up to the amount you have put in of course. While it is your money, the banks would rather you did not move it.

All of these banks have one thing in common as Daisy's story illustrates: they are concerned with receiving our money, all of it, on an ongoing basis. And they want to hold on to it for as long as possible.

Have you ever wondered why there are limits to how much money you can take out a day from an ATM machine or why they instituted a daily limit on your debit card?Granted not all accounts are created equal; some banks do give you the ability to withdraw any amount of cash you need provided you show the appropriate documents and identification card.

In simple terms, how do banks make money off of your money? Where do the debts you accumulate come from? Banks create money in the economy that technically wasn't there before by administering loans. This does not mean that banks can give out an infinite amount of loans to make more money. This practice could ruin an economy! There are some regulations set in place to control this, though as we have come to realize, these regulations can be circumvented. The Federal Reserve regulates the lending of money by setting reserve requirements that indicate the amount of money banks are allowed to lend.

Let's say you put $1,000 into your bank account into a bank account. Of that $1,000 dollars, the bank is allowed to lend out $900 dollars of the total you have put in. The Federal Reserve dictates that banks are allowed to lend out 90% of your deposit and can not touch 10% of it. The $900 from your $1,000 deposit goes back out into the economy and ends up deposited into another bank. These banks are then able to lend out 90% of the $900 that was put into the account, and on and on, creating an exponentially increasing amount of money in the economy.

Does the Federal Reserve ever change the reserve requirement? Depending on how the US economy is doing, the Federal Reserve will regulate different metrics (fed tools) to fit the economy's needs at the time. So if the Federal Reserve lowers the requirement, that means less money will be held onto, consequently pumping more money out into the economy! The fancy term for this process is called the "expansionary monetary policy".

If the federal reserve wants to slow economic growth and reduce liquidity (amount of money in the economy), they will raise the requirement so that less money gets put into the economy. The fancy term for that is called a contractionary policy. The lower the requirement, the more money banks get to make off your money because it's more money they can lend out!

Now that you understand the bank's motivation, a good step in realizing what in your system needs a change is to sit down and think about what you want. What are your dreams and goals? Don't worry about the things you have; think about the future. Is it a big house? The ability to travel the world? A spouse and kids and the whole white picket fence?

There is no wrong answer here; the only wrong answer is not doing the exercise. Until you do, you will struggle to understand how tied to your dreams your financial situation is.

As such, you will not be able to adequately place yourself within the larger structure and how to best use it to your advantage.

Your Homework?

Write down all of your dreams as you have them. Don't think of any as too outlandish or foolish—remember—you're dreaming! Let the thoughts fly and take careful action.

Now, prioritize those dreams. Which are the most important? Which are most feasible? Which would you love to do the most? Put them in the order in which you will try to attain them. Remember, we are always moving toward action—not just dreaming. You need a plan. In the case of building massive financial wealth, you need a flexible yet robust plan.

Remember the questions I asked as we began to determine if this book is for you? They were meant to lead you here. If you are starting from a vulnerable state, from the bottom, so to speak, remember that when the stakes are down, and our lives are lying in shambles, we are paradoxically awarded the ideal opportunity to start over.

Use your ill fortune as the excuse you've been waiting to walk away from that lousy job or commit to living paycheck to paycheck that is making you miserable. If you're going to be forced to start over, you might as well do it once, the right way.

LESSON LEARNED
05

CHAPTER 02

IN DEFENSE OF MASSIVE WEALTH

wish I had a money tree.

Oh, but there are so many reasons why this would be a terrible idea. For starters, a money tree would need a constant watch, caring for, and patience to maintain. These facts, coupled with the impossibility based on science alone dictates I should err on the side of caution while operating heavy machinery. But that's beside the point. I am a member of the millennial crowd; we live in a time where we are constantly reminded of the possibility of making billions overnight.

We "follow" influencers who talk about their unmatched success doing what they love. We send tweets to CEOs of corporations that started in a garage knowing very well that they are too busy jetting around to pay attention to our simpleton requests.

We vacation in Bali and watch the super-wealthy deep into their heated rooftop outdoor pools and exclaim to ourselves: "one day surely! That'll be me."

Some of us do arrive at the age where we resent those who hold the top 10% of our world's wealth. This fact begs the question then, what, if anything, is wrong with extreme wealth? We speak about the Bill Gates, Elon Musk, and Jeff Bezos of the world as if they are mystical superhumans without hearts -- just massive brains capable of computing the return on investment on their interactions with the world. We dehumanize them to the point of pushing them all into "giving back" in humanitarian aid and philanthropy. It is not without much consideration that they pour their funds and some of their friends to appease our small egos into calm.

At the risk of discounting the pleasure one receives from philanthropic activities, allow me to enlighten those who see the world with rose-colored glasses. There are three kinds of individuals who pour funds into humanitarian programs: they either want to do good, look good, or do both. In other words, the outpour of funds into these programs comes with massive advantages, whether emotional or financial.

Our entire world is managed by incentive. This morning when you woke up, what did you do? Did you log onto your computer, so you didn't get fired from your job?

Did you meet a friend who told you they had business to discuss once you were done with work? Did you exercise for an hour so you can feel better and look good overall? We are motivated by incentive, through and through.

For the people looking to give back, as the final part of their wealth management, they can be broken down into three kinds of givers:

- They want to do good: They want nothing more than to make the world a better place. They don't need the gold star or the trophy to prove it. They could give anonymously and know that they are helping other people.
- They want to look good: These are the people who want a photo of them giving. They want articles, headlines, and talk shows to note how charitable they are. There is an element of self-obsession in giving, but they are still giving something of theirs away.
- They want to do both: Lastly, some genuinely enjoy the benefits of both giving, as well as the positive press that comes from it. Corporate Social Responsibility (CSR) is significant today. Why? People care how companies choose to use their money. They want to see them be philanthropic. There's a new kind of public element to it today.

Your reasoning for being philanthropic can be any one of these three options. Sure, the most selfish option is to "look good," but at the end of the day, you are still giving nonetheless. It's both a personal and financial win for your empire as you choose to engage in philanthropic endeavors. As long as you uphold your responsibility as a wealthy financial success to do more and give back, you are defending the case for massive wealth. It's easy for those to criticize the wealthy and claim they are withholding the 99% of the country's wealth from everyone else.

Defend your claim as a wealthy person by hiring help, donating, volunteering, and giving back. When you reach this point in your wealth journey, you have officially conquered the art of amassing wealth. The best thing you can do is give it away to help the next wealth builder on the same conquest. **Remember:** you can't take it with you when you die. Once you feel like you have mastered the art of wealth-building, think about the legacy you want to leave.

Massive wealth can positively impact the world when it finds itself in the right hands.

CHAPTER 03

RESPONSIBILITY OF A WEALTH BUILDER

Did I fail to mention that Daisy is a social butterfly? She has managed to make a friend in nearly every city. Some of her friends do well for themselves; they are building massive estates even as young adults. Jake happens to be the H.E.N.R.Y. (high earner not rich yet) she reaches out to when she has a financial concern. Jake manages to save 40% of his income every month and owns a multi-family property in an upcoming town in Connecticut. While he holds his current home, he shares the mortgage payment with three roommates, making it easy for him to jet around every quarter. The great thing about Daisy's relationship with Jake is that Jake has yet to be annoyed with her incessant money-related questions.

Jake admitted to me, however, that he is tired of being the go-to financial guru of their circle of friends. He has inadvertently taken a role for his friends that he knows he cannot sustain for very long. While Jake complains about the role he plays in his friends' lives, I find myself applauding them for reaching out for advice from someone well versed enough to know they need to speak with a professional.

Jake once exclaimed: "would you ask a plumber to perform throat surgery on you?" One could easily detect a level of disappointment in his tone. "With my limited knowledge, I feel like a total scam as I ditch out advice to my friends," he continued.

Jake is correct: you would not ask directions from someone who had never been down the path you seek. He was referred to my financial advising practice precisely because he wanted to avoid making that mistake.

He actively sought books, and as soon as he realized his limitations as it pertains to the practical application of his readings, he called upon a professional.

Jake's golden rule is that if you want something, you have to live and breathe it. He did not realize as he began his journey to building wealth as the weight of responsibility to himself and those around him. That's right! Who would have thought that your growth would result in an additional burden in your life?

As you begin your ascension, several things will take place. You will first start to receive questions on how, what, when. Then, you will receive questions around exact numbers. Lastly, and this is highly dependent on your circle or community, you might begin to receive requests to share.

Do you know this Spiderman quote: "with great power comes great responsibility?" It's a relevant quote that can relate to just about everything in your life. When it comes to money— one of the most controversial assets in the world— responsibility has never been more critical. People will die today on a conquest of money. It makes the world go round, albeit in evil ways at times.

 The more money and wealth you accumulate, the higher your responsibility for managing that money.

It's not like the music videos where singers drop $100 bills off the back of their sports car while dancers twerk in the background. Wealth management, when done correctly, involves conscious effort, professional management, and removal of emotional attachment. Suddenly, when you get passionate about your money, it can control you – like a wicked ex-girlfriend or boyfriend. Don't give your money that control. Remember that YOU control it.

The responsibility of a wealth builder, is, therefore, twofold:

- **It's your responsibility to stay on top of your empire and make changes based on relevant and adequate information.**
- **It's your responsibility to do good with your wealth and leave the planet better than you found it.**

What's the point of sitting on 10 million dollars if you are never going to do anything? Now you are throwing away the power to make the world a better place. Surely you don't want to die knowing you left zero contribution behind?

The more money you own, the more options you have at your disposal. Should you invest it in the stock market, take out more insurance, buy real estate, buy a home for your parents? Be careful what you wish for, or so the adage says.

That's why you want to prepare in these early stages for a future in which you were successful in amassing wealth. What will you do then? Do you have a plan? We will discuss a succession plan for over-achievers soon enough but before we go there, I must stress the importance of your responsibility as a wealth-builder.

Do you know what can buy you happiness? A 2008 study by Harvard Business School found that giving money to someone else improved the giver's happiness more than spending it on themselves. The responsibility of someone with much money is to do good with that money.

Volunteer, fund nonprofits, donate to charities, invest in your local town, and pass it down efficiently to your heirs. Remember, when I mentioned how the circulation of money is like energy – it can be neither created nor destroyed? If you send your money back out into the cycle, it's going to come back. Be willing to let it go. The more prepared you are to take risks and A.C.T., the more rewarded you will become.

The responsibility of a wealth builder is to be a role model for the younger generations reading this today.

You cannot give what you do not have.

That said, the priority as a wealth builder is to one's self. Only then can one begin to share the knowledge and empower others through personal endeavors, civic and political activism, and philanthropic activities. However, all of this starts with prioritizing the action steps it takes to reach the end goal.

Prioritize Financial Literacy

Our schooling systems fail us tremendously when they do not provide years of comprehensive financial education. All that time we spent learning about special calculus tricks (although useful for calculus professors), could have been diverted to financial literacy.

We have millions of people every single year at the age of 18 released into the world with no idea how to: save, budget, file taxes, invest, or buy insurance. It's a recipe for disaster, coupled with the mountain of student loan debt they get to sign to ensure entry into higher education institutions.

If acquiring wealth is essential to you, it's time to take a hard look at your knowledge bank; it's time to go back to the basics and sit with your finances. It's time to mull over what they look like and what you want them to resemble.

What Does It Mean to Be Financially Literate?

Financially literate individuals technically know a fair amount regarding budgeting and setting financial goals, paying bills and saving money, managing loans and debt, credit cards and credit scores, investing, and retirement planning.

Financial literacy is not something you are "born with." It's not something more suited to one person than to another. It's something you need to make a proactive effort to include in your life, which you can start committing to today.

Here are a few ways to become financially literate on your own:

- Starting Reading: You've made a decision to do already this, which I applaud. You are well on your way to becoming financially literate, only by reading on the subject.

I recommend dedicating 1-2 hours per day to learn about financial topics so financial management can become second nature to you.

- Follow Online Publications: Subscribe to Bankrate, Student Loan Hero, MarketWatch, the Wall Street Journal, Business2Community.com to start reading about the latest financial trends. A subscription to an online publication is a great way to stay abreast of financial changes as financial norms change constantly.

- Use Financial Management Tools: You can use technology to your advantage. Check out companies like Y.N.A.B., and Personal Capital if you want to embed automation tools that generate reports for you to view. These reports will help you spot trends you can use to enhance your wealth in the future.

- Listen to Podcasts: Making time to read for 2-hours per day doesn't always pan out as we anticipate. You should subscribe to money-based podcasts you can listen to in the car or while walking to and from your place of employment. Many of these podcasts will cover budgeting, credit repair, remote work, making money on the road, and so forth. It's a free education and something you can listen to during your free time.

- Break Out of Consumer Mentalities: Part of living in America is the presence of advertisements everywhere you go. It's the sign of a thriving consumer economy. Although that is a beautiful thing, break these ad's influence over you. Understand which of your behaviors are controlled by ads, so you have more control over what you buy. Many times, we end up buying things we don't need – at all.

All of these are steps a person can take to begin the preparation towards building massive wealth. If you have zero dollars to put towards this, subscribe to magazines for free, find free ebooks, find free podcasts, and start to work on your mindset.

Note that I recommend financial literacy as a starting point for two distinct reasons. The first reason is a rather obvious one: knowledge is power. This kind of experience will equip you to ask better and more pertinent questions to the quarterback of your finances. Allow me to introduce you to acquiring a financial advisor, regardless of your current financial state. Thus, the second reason is that as an informed consumer, you can better pick said financial advisor. Let me assure you. We are not all cut from the same cloth.

Besides being financially literate, having access to your financial advisor is the most excellent decision you can make toward achieving your goal.

A financial advisor, a fiduciary, whose role is to help you make decisions, can guide you in your journey to building massive wealth. If need be, a fiduciary can go as far as helping you implement all of the strategies. Here are just a few ways in which a financial advisor can change the trajectory of your wealth:

- Better investment opportunities: Financial advisors wake up every day with one mission – to find the best investment opportunities available for their clients. Since most people aren't knowledgeable on how to invest, they will opt not to invest altogether, or fall victim to scams and activities like stock picking that can destroy your financial future.
- Get you one step ahead of inflation: Inflation, otherwise known as the gradual increase in general price levels of goods and services, goes up every year. If you have the same X dollars in your bank account, they will be worth less and less when compared to inflation over time. Therefore, if you are not keeping up with inflation rates, you are losing your hard-earned money.
- Wealth management strategies: There are multiple ways in which you can manage your wealth. Since there is no cookie-cutter default, this can make wealth management incredibly stressful for some people. Financial advisors will look at different strategies and go over which ones are most suited to your situation.

- Simplification: If you're tired of reading significant financial terms and equations that can hurt your brain, a financial advisor can shoulder some responsibility for you. They will simplify your options and present them to you in the most comfortable possible terms.

- Risk awareness and mitigation: As mentioned, there is always an element of risk when it comes to money. That's why so many people are afraid to touch their money or do anything constructive with it. Financial advisors act as a buffer between you and any bad risks that stand to offset your wealth. That's why you always want to consult with one before making any big decisions.

Your Homework?

Visualize the wealth you have created. On a piece of paper, visualize what you are able to achieve with it. Write the names of the people whose lives you have changed.

_____

_____

_____

_____

_____

CHAPTER 04

THE WEALTH BUILDER MAP FROM BIRTH TO DEATH

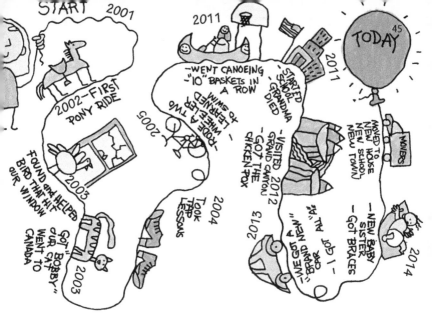

Let us evaluate the natural progression of wealth accumulation from birth to death. The section will speak primarily to the average person who has no inheritance, special trust funds, or anything else in their name. We are going to start with the value of $0, or for some, even less. Even if you have more to your name, this is still a valuable progression to follow for where you want to see your financial standing in the coming years.

So, let's dial in back to graduating from high school, or the age of 18. You probably didn't have much else on your mind but going to school, going on dates, and getting invites to the hottest parties in town. We've all been there. What should high school-you get started with a wealth builder map? You guessed it: invest.

When it comes to investing, there are two critical components to consider: risk tolerance and time on the horizon.

If you have a higher risk tolerance, you might be more willing to take a chance on risky stocks that could pay big or lose big. It depends on what you're ready to stomach. I have a reasonably high-risk tolerance. I've watched my portfolio decline and then come back, and then dip again. Reacting to these changes with zero emotion is vital.

At 18, the volatility of the stock market in the interim shouldn't matter. Your eye is on the 50-year prize, which is a long-term investing strategy. What happens to the market right now will have zero impact on what you are taking out of the stock market when you turn 65. That's the kind of mentality you will need to adopt.

Remember: the last 20 years have not exactly been mellow. There was the September 11th terrorist attack, the financial crisis of 2009, and COVID-19 in 2020. Stop looking at these events as ones that impact your worth. They are short-term hiccups that will have no bearing on your long-term gains.

With what money you do have, even if it's $20, it's time to invest at 18. It's the first thing you should do. The more you set aside at a younger age, the bigger the payout will be down the line. It's simple math.

Once you get your investments down, it's time to think about insurance.

Life insurance is that missing piece of the puzzle that will help a wealth builder balance their own retirement needs while ensuring their kids are also taken care of – it's a win-win for everyone involved. As we mentioned before, there are different kinds of life insurance. If you want to protect the money you can take out without tax, there's permanent life insurance.

If you want a policy that pays out to your family in the event of death, there is term life insurance.

If you are young, loading up on term life insurance makes sense. It's cheap for young, healthy people, and you will have fewer assets when you are old. You will need more life insurance now to ensure your family is taken care of should anything happen.

As time progresses and you build your wealth, minimizing tax liabilities will be next on the list of to-dos. You have now invested in both stocks and insurance. Good. Taxes can creep up on you if you don't strategically maneuver your money.

Since life insurance payouts are not taxable, they are a critical instrument in transferring wealth to your kids without paying taxes.

You can also switch over to permanent life insurance once your wealth has grown substantially. But, until them, term life insurance is what makes the most sense.

The D Word

Debt carries a negative connotation that has many adults convinced it's a "bad" thing they should avoid whenever possible. However, some debt is not bad at all – it's healthy and a natural part of building your wealth. If you see carrying debt as a failure, you will end up veering off the course of amassing wealth the right way.

If you carry debt, it means you had to borrow money to invest in something bigger than your life. You had to take out a loan for a car, a home, or your education. As we know now, education leads to knowledge, which is one of the major precursors to expanded and fortified wealth.

However, not all debt is created equal. Taking out loans is one thing – amassing credit card debt for consumer spending is BAD. It means you are spending money you don't have on items that are not important for growing your wealth.

Taking on $50,000 in debt to complete a master's degree is much different from buying four Gucci purses that you "want" for the time being.

Mind you, taking on debt is a risk, no doubt. If you do it wisely, you can use it as a tool to increase your overall wealth. Reel in debt if possible and don't take out four different $50,000 loans in one year. You need to be able to see the light at the end of the tunnel. We can only mentally handle so much debt without feeling hopeless or unable to pay it back. This can impact your mindset, causing you to start closing in on all of your hopes and dreams.

Income

A big part of amassing wealth as a first-generation wealth builder is having an income of some sort. To invest in all of these great options and pay off your debt, you need a flow of money coming into your bank accounts. You are going to need to work hard – it's the name of the game. Let's say you start a new job that pays $45,000 per year.

That's not too shabby! Considering the average American household income is $61,937 per year, 45k is a respectable figure at a young age.

The problem is that this might not be enough money to afford rent, utilities, transportation, saving, and investing. If you're like me, you want to start amassing that wealth, and you want to do it today.

The beauty of the internet today is that you can secure a side hustle if you want! A side hustle is something you do "on the side" to make some cash. It can be freelancing online, working as an Uber driver, offering consultations to clients, and social media management. This will enable you to earn more money and diversify your income if something happens to your job.

For many people today, their side hustles become so lucrative that they quit their day jobs to pursue it full time. We all know that diversifying your investments is essential, right? Well, what about your income? It's the same kind of concept!

And, no one said you needed to stop at just one side hustle. Why not have a few? If you're a freelance writer, why not sign up on two freelancing sites instead of one? Never put all of your eggs in one basket – you'll be protected by unexpected shifts and changes in the economy and job market.

Your Family

Now that you have rounded out investing in yourself, the final part of being a wealth builder is to consider the human capital in your life. By social capital, I mean your family. What is life without family? Is any of this worth it if you don't have people that you love at the end of the day? Of course not!

By amassing your wealth now, you can provide a safety net for your family members. Unforeseen events happen. People get sick, injured, or lose their jobs. I want to be able to cover expenses for both my kids and parents when they need it. I want to be able to buy a home for my parents to retire because they deserve it. This home can also double as one of my investments, make my parents happy, and help me grow my net-worth.

Open a college fund for your kid the day they are born. Contribute to it as much as you can. Invest in their future so that they can invest in yours. Seeing money as a "competitive" commodity within a family is a waste of your time and life. Investing in the people you love is an investment in your life, too. That's how you round out your wealth builder map from birth to death.

CHAPTER 05

THE WEALTH BUILDER MINDSET

> "Your brain is a super computer; your self talk is the programming."

You cannot throw a rock on or off social media without hitting a motivational speaker. Motivation is as it appears big business. The reason for this is half the battle to accomplishing any given goal is in your head. Some say you must visualize your goal; others say you must speak it into existence. What they are all saying is that you must learn to control your self-talk. If your self-talk is the programming that gives you strength or the audacity to dream up something huge, you will do well to invest your time in some great motivational tools. Professional motivators, as I call them, rely heavily on their accomplishments to entice the feeling.

The question is, however, how does one ensure these so-called accomplishments are real and authentic? Moreover, what makes their journey adaptable to the rest of us? The lack of adaptability is why some follow the same prescribed plan and might do well, while others may fail miserably. The element of luck remains responsible for the discrepancy in result.

That said, the first place to start with everything discussed so far is indeed the mindset. You can't reach for the stars, achieve your goals, amass wealth, and give back without having the right mindset. For so many people, their mindsets ruin their chances before they even begin. Whether you learned negative self-talk from your parents, were bullied, or you've had a hard life, that kind of defeatist mindset will never be conducive to building a healthy financial life for yourself.

Remember: no one ever said this life was going to be easy. Anything worth having takes work. Nothing worth having is handed easily to people.

It all starts with a willingness to try. That person in your hometown is criticizing you on Facebook for trying to make something of yourself.

They are only doing it because they are projecting their fears. People are afraid to fail. I bet you are, too! Who wants to feel like a public failure for everyone to ridicule?

No one. We'd instead stick to the status quo than rock the boat, only for other people.

Spoiler alert: the most prominent lessons are in failures!

As Thomas A. Edison famously said, "I have not failed. I've just found 10,000 ways that won't work."

The more you fail, the more you will learn about what works, what doesn't work, and what you need to try the second, third, or fourth time. The billionaires of our world didn't just waltz out of bed and hit a perfect 3-pointer every time. They failed too many times to count. We fixate on the successes and fail to realize the work that went on behind the scenes.

For these people, success didn't just "happen." They weren't lucky, no matter what you tell yourself. Even if they were given $1 million as a child, if they grew it to $1 billion, they put some hard work into that equation. The American Dream is still available to those who pursue it – but it's not a given. It's the product of blood, sweat, tears, and plenty of failure.

You have to be shameless and not fearful. The more you achieve for yourself, the more critics are going to criticize you behind your back. It's human nature. They are merely jealous of you and the fact that you are trying to achieve your goals! You are fearless, and they wish they could be that fearless, too.

The aforementioned brings me to the discussion of goals and goal-setting. Lofty goals will never get you to your destination. Telling yourself, "I want to be a millionaire," means nothing unless there is a blueprint roadmap for getting there. How do you plan to become a millionaire? You need to sit down and create SMART goals: specific, measurable, attainable, relevant, and time-bound. Each goal needs to have all of these details described so you can concoct how you are going to make it happen.

Dreaming is good, but doing is even better.

And the best news of all is: you don't have to do it alone! We often assume that the life of a business person is a lonely one. Yes, it's lonely at the top, but the food tastes so much better.

These people, however, didn't get to the top alone. That's why who you choose to associate with is just as important as what you do. And I am not just talking about friends. I am talking about whom you date, whom you choose as mentors, and whom you partner with in business. You are an average of the five closest people in your life — what kind of average are you staring at today? Is it one that inspires pride?

Sometimes, to get ahead, we need to shed the dead weight of the past. People can serve a purpose for a specific amount of time, but that doesn't mean they will always be able to help you. If your friends are still unhappy and judging others, it might be time to find people that inspire you.

You need this kind of inspiration because the road to financial success is going to be challenging. No one is going to set you up and do it for you. Everyone is worried about their financial adventure. Sure, they can inspire you and help you maintain a positive mindset – but they can't seize that financial freedom you seek on your behalf. That's up to you, which is why a victimhood mentality will never work. It would help to take responsibility for where you are and where you want to go. Just think of how powerful that is?

Stop concerning yourself with how the public sees you and your journey.

Entrepreneurship, although sexy to tell someone at a networking event, is not that glamorous. It's a lot of late nights, no days off, stress, and unpredictability. The things we romanticize the most are often never as they seem. Just about every children's book and Disney movie has taught us that since we were little.

Analyzing these kinds of romantic endeavors can cloud your ability to see clearly. Over-analysis leads to paralysis.

If you spend all of your time obsessing over the tiniest of details, you will never be able to see the big picture right before you very eyes. It's the deception of picking the prettiest rose in the garden as you fail to realize you are standing on top of the X for the treasure chest. What's worth more – one rose or buried treasure? To get to the cache, you need to be able to see it first. Let go of perfectionism – it doesn't exist.

Changing your mindset won't happen overnight. But, committing yourself to see the glass half full is a journey you can start today. You only have one life to live – how are you living your life? Are you happy? Are you taking risks? Are you surrounding yourself with the right people? If not, the good news is that you can start doing all of these things today!

CHAPTER 06

UNDERSTANDING YOUR
ECONOMIC VALUE:

YOUR
STARTING
POINT

usually work with single individuals; "couples are traditionally difficult to work with because they did not do the preliminary work before getting married," I explain to the lovely pair. They look at me perplexed, smile, and take the seats I was showing them. I can tell they are burning to ask more questions on my abrupt statement. I usually start my initial meetings, but lately, it has been as if the creator has been putting words in my mouth.

I swiftly change course and welcome them to our place of business. Today is all about you, I exclaim. So, get comfortable because we are going to discuss your financial goals as individuals and a pair. "Do not worry so as not to offend your partner; we are here to learn and grow together." The more I talk, the more impressed they seem, and while that should flatter, I find it scary.

We have a thirty-eight-year-old woman married to a fifty-three-year-old male. They have three children together, one of which has a developmental disability. The husband, up until three months ago, was the sole provider. They have gone from being a single paycheck to a dual-income household. They should be elated, but they are more concerned than ever.

Before I go into the rigorous process, I allow them to discuss some of the issues they face about their finances. The couple announces that one of the boys has a developmental disability. From the parents' account, he will always require support, be it financial or mental. While there are state-funded programs for this kind of situation, they are not confident their child would qualify, and if so, if it would be enough.

With that worry at the forefront of their minds, they are also concerned with the wife's expensive taste and incessant shopping. She will run us to the ground with this lousy habit, announces the husband.

Ah! There it is, he had no clue that mommy loved her far too occasional retail therapy upon getting married. Careful is a non-judgmental environment, so we will refrain from commenting on how meaningful such a conversation is, considering that ninety percent of marriages fail due to financial issues.

As we continue our deep dive into their financial habits, we uncover that the wife entrusts the husband with saving for the family unit. At the onset of the meeting, she boasted how well her husband understands personal finance and has been doing a fantastic job saving for the family. She recounts, providing him with her full paycheck to stay away from her funds and keep more. While I trust everything that comes out of one's mouth, I verify everything. I gather all sorts of statements, including savings and loans. Through the simple verification process, we uncover the savings account is blank. After three months of saving, she expected to have at least seventeen thousand dollars in their savings account. At the time of the meeting, there were three.

We plow ahead without jumping to conclusions. I remind them that this is the first step to understand themselves better as it pertains to money and to start establishing good money habits. They acquiesce, albeit reluctantly, as they realized they have more to gain by working together – with a professional – than alone.

We begin the process by educating the parties. We start with the foundation of any substantial financial house **(Figure 1)**. We start by discussing how one builds or grows his or her economic value. In other words, we discuss the different aspects of a financial house, contributing to one's net worth.

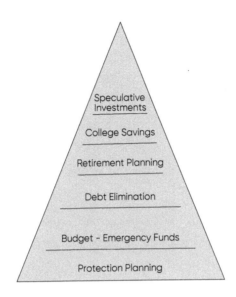

As you see in Figure 1, the foundation of any solid financial plan is protection planning (Disability Insurance, Life Insurance, Mortgage Insurance, Car Insurance). This is followed by your cash reserves or emergency funds. Once you have saved up enough for a rainy day, you should work towards eliminating debt. From there, we focus our attention solely on retirement planning, although most working adults should be contributing in some form towards their retirement. Once you have a family, you should tackle college savings plans. It is important to focus on this aspect after retirement planning considering your child can take a loan to go to college while you cannot borrow to retire. Speculative investments only become a priority after all these plans are put in place.

So, take stock of your own plan as it stands, where are you in building your own financial house? Are you well on the way to be minted? Our goal is to come up with A plan that transcends all uncertainties that life can throw at you.

The tool that helps advisors gather the appropriate information to begin this planning process, fact-finder - a series of questions that help them collect information unique to your situation.

The objective is to come up with a plan to add at least $1M dollars to your net worth in year one. (At least, that is my pledge to my clients).

Why do we talk about planning so extensively? You see, there are different types of people when it comes to financial planning. I will first establish the different categories and offer you a new path to massive wealth.

The first category of people do not plan their finances. The results of not planning can be devastating. People who do not plan tend to live day by day and may lose control over their financial lives. They become vulnerable to the events and circumstances that surround them. In a complex society such as ours, people who do not plan have less chance for financial security and the peace of mind it brings.

This category is then followed by the occasional planners. Occasional Planning is how many people make their money decisions.

This type of planning usually keeps people one step behind where they should and could be. Occasional planners are part of the do-it-yourself" clan and do not understand the importance of having professional assistance given on a timely basis therefore they tend not to reach their full financial potential.

Another group subscribes to needs planning. Needs-based planning focuses on meeting needs such as saving for a house, tuition costs, retirement income, paying estate taxes, disability income needs. This type of decision making usually takes place when the need is present. It can be said to be reactive versus proactive.

Lastly, most financial advisors promote financial planning, which focuses on meeting predetermined needs and goals. The process used in financial planning often involves number crunching and mathematical variables such as interest rates, investment rates of return in income tax rates and future income needs. Financial planning focuses additional money is required to obtain a predetermined fixed need or goal.

I subscribe to the notion of holistic financial planning. This involves the understanding and application of two distinct concepts: maintenance of a sound financial house and incremental growth of your net worth. Keeping these two in order will help ensure maximum output.

Think of yourself as a tangible item for a moment. You, yes, you have economic value to your person; your greatest asset is your ability to create income. The things you own, the thoughts in your head, and the assets you have created are related to your value. The same goes for your liabilities – the things you owe on, the mistakes you've made, and the inhibitions that keep you back from your potential are subtracted against your value.

Why bother going through this kind of equation to come to a final value? Well, this kind of equation paints a picture of your financial health. And, it does so pretty quickly. Should your liabilities outweigh your assets, then you have some problems. You will need to balance the other side of the equation to get back to good financial standing.

Your economic value is the same as your net worth. Your net worth is everything you own of significance minus what you owe in debts. These assets can include your investments, your homes, another real estate, and anything else of value. Your liabilities are typically your car loans, your mortgage, and your student loan debt.

Your Homework?

Complete the workbook that follows this chapter. If you would rather make life difficult for yourself, pick up a new notebook and let's get started!

How can you go about calculating this value in a simple, easy-to-process way? Let's check it out:

- Make a list of your assets: Spend just one hour of your retirement savings, your current checking and savings account balances, any bonds you might have, the total value of stock holdings you have, your home, and your cars. Some of these will require you to make an estimate. Sites like Zillow or Redfin can be helpful for that. Add it all up and get a total.
- Make a list of your debts: It's time to look at the loans. Your credit card balances, personal loans, student loans, mortgage, and auto loans. Need to all be added up. Get your total for this figure.
- Subtract: Subtract your loans from your assets.

If you don't like what you see, you have two options to change your value: you can increase your assets or decrease your debts. If you can do both of these things simultaneously, you will notice a significant change in this figure in just weeks.

To stay on top of this figure and where you presently stand, I would calculate your net worth every month. It should be a goal of yours to increase your net worth over the previous month, even if it's ever-so-slightly.

Once you go through this math, the lists, and the subtracting, you should know your economic value. We all have to start somewhere. Don't beat yourself up over beginning with a figure that you find to be less-than-exciting. It's merely your starting point for where you want to go. Set a goal for how much you want your net worth to change month after month.

A secure financial life does not happen by accident. Remember, a sound plan can add more to your net worth than a lifetime of work.

Accumulating wealth for financial security is a goal that requires planning as well as self-discipline. We alluded to this fact before: financial security means different things to different people. What does it mean to you? Is it enough money to pursue your dreams? Whatever financial security means to you, it begins with a plan for accumulating wealth. But with every plan, you must determine your starting point.

Unfortunately, Americans have one of the lowest savings rates in the industrialized world.

Couple this unwillingness or inability to save with spiraling college costs and the current uncertainty about Social Security, many of us will face a severe cash shortfall when it may be needed the most, as we saw with the coronavirus outbreak.

Take a second to think about what's holding you back. Maybe you're hesitant because of market conditions? Given the current investment arena, this is a very natural reaction. Depending on your investment goals, however, it may also be something that you should re-evaluate. Perhaps the market is not where you should be, especially as you begin your journey. That said, consider the following:

1

Market volatility is needed and somewhat necessary. Without periodic fluctuations, the equity markets could potentially be closed to the average investor. For example, if stock prices only went up, soon only the wealthy could afford to invest.

2

Long-term investing requires a long-term mindset. Stay the course with your investment strategy and try to avoid changing midstream because of market conditions.

Those who continue a steady investment program, mainly when the markets are down, actually have the opportunity to purchase high-quality investments, only at a much lower cost.

Do you think that you have plenty of time "down the road" to begin saving? Realize that the longer you wait, the harder it will be to find the money you'll need to set aside to meet your accumulation goals - and the cost of waiting can be steep. As most people think about accumulating wealth, they also think about when and how they'd like to retire. The typical 45-year old married couple in the United States will have only a portion of what they'll need at retirement to maintain their current lifestyle. Where will the rest of the money come from?

Do you think Social Security will be the answer? If the experts are right, you better think again. Assuming Social Security is still solvent when you retire, it will pay only a small percentage of your pre-retirement income.

For example, if your 2011 salary is $200,000, your annual Social Security benefit would be about $29,400. Could you live on this amount? Think about when you spend the most money. Is it on the weekends or during the week when you are at work? During retirement, every day is the weekend. Would you agree then you would need more money at retirement and not less?

Wealth Accumulation Strategies

There are many ways to begin a wealth accumulation strategy, but there are fundamental principles for any successful program:

1 Save money regularly and consistently. Develop a sound plan and stick to it over the long term.

Most experts agree you should save at least 10% of your earnings, consistently and throughout your earning years.

None of this is going to be easy – nothing worth having ever is. That's why it's important to approach all of this with a humanistic mindset.

You are still a person that needs to enjoy the fruits of your labor. If you try and save every last penny without allotting yourself any money to enjoy a few meals out per month, etc., you are going to burn out. I have seen it happen.

That said, you must still pay yourself first. What does this mean?

It means you need to set yourself up for success by budgeting for your happiness. You need to set aside some money for your short-term to mid-term goals.

While it can serve these purposes, this does not necessarily translate into money for meals out, movie tickets, or a trip every few months, or even that purse or bag you've been wanting, etc. The point is no matter your income, you can have it all with a little budgeting and planning.

"Save by design; not by default"

LESSON LEARNED 13

You must learn to save by design, not by default. You will start to hate the process and throw out your newfound literacy altogether if you do not adopt a mindset in which you start to love and appreciate this new kind of financial chapter for your future.

Additionally, to develop a sound strategy and stick with it, start by taking these steps (See the Minted Workbook):

a) Define your long-term goals. Where do you want to be 10, 20, or even 30 years from now?

b) Know your time horizon. How much time does your money have to grow before you need it?

c) Know your risk tolerance. Are you willing to ride out fluctuations in the value of your investments to potentially achieve higher long-term goals, or do you need to see regular and steady growth?

2 Diversify. Spread your investments out over several asset classes or financial buckets to help protect against the normal fluctuations in each class (also called Asset Allocation). There is no assurance that a diversified portfolio will achieve a better return than a non-diversified portfolio.

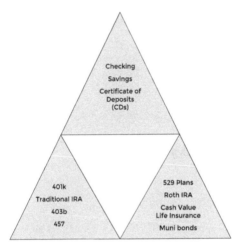

Checking
Savings
Certificate of
Deposits
(CDs)

401k
Traditional IRA
403b
457

529 Plans
Roth IRA
Cash Value
Life Insurance
Muni bonds

Financial Vehicles to Help Achieve Asset Allocation

Annuities

Grow tax-deferred. Fixed annuities offer a guaranteed rate of return.

Mutual Funds

Pooled funds that are professionally managed, allowing low initial investments and a wide range of growth objectives.

Stocks and Bonds

A range of investment objectives can be met purchasing the stock of various companies, and by purchasing bonds issued by the government, municipalities, or some U.S. corporations.

Cash Value Life Insurance

Cash values can be borrowed against tax-free to help fund your child's education or supplement retirement income. Plus, cash values generally are not included as an asset for the purposes of calculating financial aid for college.*

Coverdell IRAs

(formerly known as Educational IRAs) - Eligible parents, grandparents, and others may make annual non-deductible contributions to Coverdell IRAs for a child under 18, subject to certain maximum limits.

529 Programs

Based on the Internal Revenue Code section that created qualified tuition programs, were designed to help meet the increasing cost of education. Generally permits larger annual contributions then the Coverdell IRA. However, certain limits still apply.

Certain limitations may apply to loans or withdrawals. Policy loans and withdrawals will reduce the death benefit and cash values, and may be taxable under certain circumstances.

3 *Create an Emergency Fund*

This emergency fund should be liquid and cover about three to six-months of standard living expenses. That's the kind of fund businesses are going through right now as we enter month four of partial shutdown. Coronavirus has highlighted that this emergency fund is not only necessary – it's paramount.

If you are single, or you exist in a single-income family, I would recommend extending that emergency fund up to 10-12 months of expenses. Having a year's worth of funds at your disposal provides immediate security to both you and your family. It's especially important if you should lose your job or fall into an unexpected sickness that can take more than a month to accommodate.

Your Homework?

Find that extra money in the budget. **Here are some ideas:**

1. Examine your spending. Write down every dollar you spend for one month. Are there places you could cut back?

2. Reduce your debt. You may be able to save hundreds, even thousands of dollars in interest every year by consolidating debt and paying off high-interest debt as soon as you can.

3. Pay credit card balances every month. Ignore the minimum payment and pay as much as you can. Why keep paying high finance charges when you do not have a zero APR card?

4. Pay yourself first. Save or invest at least 10% of your earnings starting this month. Use payroll deduction or automatic transfers directly from your checking account. Reinvest the earnings or dividends.

5. Take advantage of tax-deferred saving
   Your assets will accumulate faster if a portion of the gain does not have to be paid out in taxes. If I could, I would name my child Roth IRA. Well, I may be kidding but I do love the tax-deferred benefits associated with Roths. As long as you still qualify, make contributions towards your Roth and thank me later for the tax-deferred growth on your dollars.

Alternatively, and even concurrently, you can utilize life insurance policies to enjoy similar tax benefits. Beware that variable annuities and variable universal life insurance are subject to market fluctuations and may lose value.

Take advantage of dollar cost averaging. While dollar cost averaging does not assume a profit or protect against a loss, it can help you reduce the risk of market fluctuations by investing systematically over time. Instead of trying to invest only at the "right time," make a commitment to invest a set amount of money every month and stick to your plan - regardless of what the markets are doing.

> "The trouble for most people is they don't decide to get wealthy, they just dream about it." – Michael Masters

5 Intelligent Ways to Stay On Top of Your Finances

This list is by no means inclusive – there are many other ways to accumulate wealth. But, here are some starter ideas:

Automate Your Finances:
According to self-made millionaire David Bach, if your financial plan isn't on auto-pilot, then you are doing something wrong.

Sending your money automatically to investment accounts, retirement accounts, etc. will enable you to build wealth effortlessly. As Bach wrote in his book The Automatic Millionaire, automated payments is "the one step that virtually guarantees that you won't fail financially." He said you will never be tempted to skimp on savings again because you won't even realize the money is leaving your paycheck and depositing directly into your accounts. If you can't see it happening, you can't lament the "loss" of that spendable income every month. How do you make this happen? Simply link your accounts and hook up direct payment into your desired accounts. Meet with your financial advisor every few months to adjust the amount that is being deposited. Enjoy more free time you once spent analyzing where your money should be going!

2 Do Something with Your Spare Change:

No, you do not need a lot of money to get started with wealth building. Micro-investing is an effective way to grow what money you do have. There are apps out there today, like Acorns, where you can invest your spare change as you go. Let's say you have $9 leftover in your personal spending allotment at the end of the month.

You can put that $9 towards investments that, if invested at age 24, can be worth tens of thousands by the time you are age 60. For this strategy, start sooner than later and take full advantage of a miracle financial tool: compounded interest.

3 **Automate Your Daily Purchases:**

Do you spend $5 on a cup of coffee every day? You know that can add up to $150 per month, or thousands per year. Although you should never have to forgo your cup of Starbucks coffee, why not make it at home? Take time to find a brand you love and invest in quality creamer. This will not only save you time in the morning, but it will add up to tens of thousands over the course of your life. In this case, you can have your cake, and eat it, too.

4 **Write Down Your Money Goals:**

Our brains work best when we have actual goals we want to achieve. Thinking that you want to "save" and "grow" money isn't enough. You need to actually write down how much you want to try and save this year. When you have that numerical value, you can break it down per month and use your apps to help you achieve that number. Talk with your financial advisor about these goals so they can provide valuable tips and suggestions for making it happen.

Save Unexpected Cash:

If you receive a bonus or some side income from personal jobs you do during your free time, don't take that money and blow it. So many people assume a bonus is something they can drop on an extraneous purchase. Since you weren't expecting this cash, don't just launch it back out into the universe. Put it towards your saving goals so you can reach those goal markers that much sooner. This will, in turn, motivate you to work harder so more of this unexpected money appears.

YOUR DREAMS & GOALS

IDENTIFY YOUR LIFE STAGE AND CHOICES

Knowing where you are in life today and identifying where you want to be tomorrow is critical to living and maintaining the life you cherish. Review Chapter 6 of Get Minted! to start thinking about how your life's story is unfolding. Identify your life stages and record it below.

Then list your life choice like your marital and family status, education and career, home and lifestyle. List things you enjoy doing and things you are passionate about.

Finally list the financial objectives that you've accomplished in your current and prior life stages and the financial objectives you still need to address.

YOUR LIFE STAGE	YOUR LIFE CHOICES	YOUR FINANCIAL OBJECTIVES
		THOSE YOU'VE ADDRESSED:
		THOSE TO ADDRESS:

YOUR **DREAMS & GOALS**

VISUALIZE AND PRIORITIZE YOUR FUTURE

The journey toward achieving your dreams is best accomplishes by taking smaller, more manageable steps toward specific goals. Below you can list your short-term, long-term and retirement goals. As you set your goals, ask yourself the following questions to determine the likehood that you'll achieve them. If you answer no to either question, you may want to list it as a stretch ambition below.

1. **ARE YOU WILLING TO DO WHATEVER IS NECESSARY TO ACCOMPLISH THIS GOAL?**
   (Willing- no matter how to difficult, long it may take, or what the level of personal sacrifice)

2. **ARE YOU ABLE TO DO WHATEVER IS NECESSARY TO ACCOMPOLISH THIS GOAL?**
   (Able-have or able to obtain the capabilities, talents and resources needed)

REACHING YOUR GOALS

SHORT-TERM GOALS
In the next five years my top
financial priorities are:

Possible obstacles or
changes are:

LONG-TERM GOALS
Before I retire, I'd like to accomplish:

A major purchase I'd like to make is:

Possile obstacles or changes are:

RETIREMENT GOALS:
I plan to completely retire at age: *(enter age for both, if planning with a partner)*

I'd like to leave a legacy or inheritance to:

My top priorities for retirement are:

My Stretch ambition in life is to:

CALCULATING **YOUR WORTH**

TRACK THE GROWTH OF YOUR ASSETS

HOUSEHOLD ASSETS	VALUE		VALUE
Saving account(s)	$	All IRA(s)	$
Checking account(s)	$	Cash value in life insurance	
CDs/money mkt.		policies	$
account(s)	$	House/residence equity	$
Brokerage account(s)	$	Other Property equity	$
Investments /Securities	$	Car(s)	$
Pensions/Profit Sharing	$	Personal property	$
Retirement plan account(s)	$	**TOTAL**	$

HOUSEHOLD LIABILITIES	AMOUNT OWED	TERM	INTEREST RATE
Mortgage #1	$		
Mortgage #2	$		
Loan(s)	$		
Car loan(s)	$		
Credit card debt	$		
Student loan(s)	$		
Taxes (Federal/state)	$		
All Insurance payments	$		

TOTAL

HOUSEHOLD ASSETS $	−	HOUSEHOLD LIABILITY $	=	YOUR NET WORTH $

ASSETS

HARD ASSETS

- Cars, boats, bicycles, RVs
- Home, vacation and rental properties
- Expensive equipment
- Jewelry, furs, fine art, valuable collections and antiques

SOFT ASSETS

- Cash in savings, money market accounts, permanent life insurance policy and CDs
- Investments in annuities, bonds, stock and mutual funds
- Money in your 401(k)s, IRAs and pension plans

LONG & SHORT TERM LIABILITIES

Liabilities include the total amount you owe on:

- Mortgages
- Home equity loans
- Student's loans
- Personal Loans
- Credit card debt
- Cars, boat and other valuable 'toys'
- Expensive equipment, jewelry, furs, collectibles
- Substantial amount owed to family or friends

NET WORTH

GOALS

1. Your Net Worth is a positive number.
2. Your Net Worth grows each year.

DAY TO DAY FINANCES

MONTHLY FINANCE EXAMPLES

INCOME

- Salaries, bonuses, commissions
- Dividend payments
- Trust distributions
- Social Security
- Rental income
- Child support
- Alimony payment
- Unemployment checks

TIPS FOR BUDGETING AND SAVING

Save before spending through automatic payroll deductions or transfers.

Prioritize your debt repayment by paying off highest interest debt first.

Take advantage of tax deferred savings so your money works harder for you.

SAVINGS

- Savings Accounts and Cash Value from Life Insurance
- Retirement Plan Contributions
- Automatic deposits into brokerage accounts

DEBT

- Mortgage or Rent
- Car
- Credit Cards
- Loans

- Utilities
- Child Care
- Insurance
- Auto Repairs

- Transportation
- Food
- Entertainment
- Taxes

MONTHLY EXPENSES WORKSHEET

HOME

Mortgage/Rent	$	Internet	$
Condo/Association Dues	$	Cable/Satellite	$
Insurance	$	Phone (Mobile/Land Line)	$
Gas/Oil (Heat)	$	Water/Sewer/Trash	$
Electricity	$	Other	$

PERSONAL

Life Insurance	$	Other Education	$
Health Insurance	$	Clothing	$
Dental Insurance	$	Personal Supplies	$
Prescriptions	$	Laundry/Dry Cleaning	$
Long-term Care Insurance	$	Club/Membership Dues	$
School Tuition/Fees	$	Entertainment	$
Student Loan(s)	$	Other	$

CARS

Gas	$	**MISCELLANEOUS**	
Insurance	$	Gifts/Donations	$
Service/Repairs	$	Credit Cards	$
Parking/Garage	$	Loans	$
Other	$	Taxes (Federal/State)	$
		Savings	$
		Other	$

FOOD

Groceries	$	Dining Out/Restaurants	$
Other			$

RATIOS

DEBT-TO-INCOME
$ _Monthly debt_ ÷ $ _Monthly income_ = % _Your ratio_

SAVING-TO-INCOME
$ _Monthly debt_ ÷ $ _Monthly income_ = % _Your ratio_

EMERGENCY FUND
$ _Monthly debt_ × $ 6 Months = $ _Funds needed_

CALCULATING **YOUR WORTH**

TRACK THE GROWTH OF YOUR ASSETS

HOUSEHOLD ASSETS	VALUE		VALUE
Saving account(s)	$	All IRA(s)	$
Checking account(s)	$	Cash value in life insurance	
CDs/money mkt.		policies	$
account(s)	$	House/residence equity	$
Brokerage account(s)	$	Other Property equity	$
Investments /Securities	$	Car(s)	$
Pensions/Profit Sharing	$	Personal property	$
Retirement plan account(s)	$	**TOTAL**	$

HOUSEHOLD LIABILITIES	AMOUNT OWED	TERM	INTEREST RATE
Mortgage #1	$		
Mortgage #2	$		
Loan(s)	$		
Car loan(s)	$		
Credit card debt	$		
Student loan(s)	$		
Taxes (Federal/state)	$		
All Insurance payments	$		

TOTAL

HOUSEHOLD ASSETS $	-	HOUSEHOLD LIABILITY $	=	YOUR NET WORTH $

ASSETS

HARD ASSETS

- Cars, boats, bicycles, RVs
- Home, vacation and rental properties
- Expensive equipment
- Jewelry, furs, fine art, valuable collections and antiques

SOFT ASSETS

- Cash in savings, money market accounts, permanent life insurance policy and CDs
- Investments in annuities, bonds, stock and mutual funds
- Money in your 401(k)s, IRAs and pension plans

LONG & SHORT TERM LIABILITIES

Liabilities include the total amount you owe on:

- Mortgages
- Home equity loans
- Student's loans
- Personal Loans
- Credit card debt
- Cars, boat and other valuable 'toys'
- Expensive equipment, jewelry, furs, collectibles
- Substantial amount owed to family or friends

NET WORTH

GOALS

1. Your Net Worth is a positive number.
2. Your Net Worth grows each year.

NORA A. GAY

WHAT WILL YOUR RETIREMENT LOOK LIKE?

Assessing your feelings about retirement will go a long way toward achieving your goals.

RETIREMENT PLANNING SELF ASSESSMENT

PLEASE RESPOND TO EACH STATEMENT BY INDICATING YOUR DEGREE OF AGREEMENT OR DISAGREEMENT.	STRONGLY AGREE	SOMEWHAT AGREE	NOT SURE	SOMEWHAT DISAGREE	STRONGLY DISAGREE
I expect to outlive my average life expectancy by a number of years.					
I want to take full advantage of the early years of retirement to live life to the fullest.					
I believe I will collect most of the Social Security benefits that I am owned.					
I don't want to spend all the money I have on my retirement; I want to leave something to my heirs.					
I am concerned about living alone at older ages.					
I like the idea of working part-time in retirement in a job or field that I might enjoy.					
I want the early years of my retirement to be easy, relaxed and worry-free.					
Health issues could play a major part in how I approach retirement planning.					
I worry a lot about the possibility that my assets or income might run out in retirement.					
I worry about the impact of inflation on my retirement income.					
I worry that I will make big mistakes in important decisions, such as a rollover.					
After retirement starts, I should preserve my assets by not taking much investment risk.					
I worry about paying for health care costs in retirement.					
I expect to live in a different house or community during most of retirement than where I live now.					

NORA A. GAY

CLARIFY **THE RETIREMENT YOU WANT**

HOW LONG MUST YOUR RETIREMENT LAST?

From birth the average life expectancy in 2012 for males is age 75 . 81 years and for females is age 81 . 73 years - *Source: U.S Census Bureau, International Date Base, April 2009.*

LONGEVITY SCORECARD

QUESTIONS	A	B	C
Which of your parents lived to age 70 (or probably will)?	Both	One	None
How many incidents of cardiovascular problems has your extended family experienced?	None	One	More than one
How often do you exercise vigorously?	Regularly	Occasionally	Almost Never
How is your blood pressure?	Low or normal	A little high	Very high
Have you ever suffered a serious illness involving heart, liver, kidneys, lungs, or other major functions?	No	One, minor	More than once, or major
Are you a smoker?	No	Light	Heavy
Are you a drinker?	No	Modest	Heavy
How is your weight in proportion to your height?	Average or below	A little high	Quite high
How stressful is (was) your line of work?	Not at all	Modest	Heavy
How would you describe your diet?	All the right stuff	I try but snack	All the wrong stuff
How is the air and water quality where you live?	Seat belt and air bags	Seat belt or air bags but not both	Nothing between me & the windshield
	Great	Average	Poor

TOTAL ANSWERS IN EACH COLUMN			
MULTIPLY TOTALS	x 2	x 2	x 2
TOTAL POINTS			

ADD TOTAL NUMBER OF ANSWERS IN A,B & C. THIS IS YOU LONGEVITY SCORE. [   ] *Your Longevity Score*

IF YOUR LONGEVITY SCORE IS...	YOU MIGHT REASONABLY EXPECT...
20 - 24	To live at least 6-10 years beyond normal life expectancy.
15 - 19	To live 1-5 years beyond normal life expectancy.
8 - 14	To live about average life expectancy.
Less than 8	To live less than average life expectancy.

TAKE CHARGE OF YOUR FINANCIAL FUTURE

In order to properly protect your loved ones, you must consider the full value of your contributions to your household. The Charles Schwab Calculator is a unique tool that allows you to calculate your true economic value, including salary and often-overlooked or hard-to-value contributions like budgeting and managing home and family.

Go to *https://www.schwabmoneywise.com/public/file/P-4038856* to determine your full economic value and the life insurance amount needed and enter those numbers in the boxes below:

1. **ANNUAL ECONOMIC VALUE** $
   (Includes Occupational & Non-Occupation Related Value)

2. **MINIMUM AMOUNT OF LIFE INSURANCE THAT YOU MAY NEED** $

3. **QUALIFYING AMOUNT OF LIFE INSURANCE** $

THOSE AFFECTED BY MY FINANCIAL DECISIONS:

NAME	AGE	RELATIONSHIP

POLICIES CURRENTLY IN PLACE

1. **FACE VALUE OF LIFE POLICIES OWNED** $

2. **DISABILITY: % OF SALARY PAID** **. LENGTH OF COVERAGE IS** **DAYS/MONTHS.**

3. **LONG-TERM CARE: INDEMNITY AMOUNT** $ **. LENGTH OF CONFINEMENT IS** **DAYS/MONTHS.**

CHAPTER 07

OPPORTUNITIES IN
UNCERTAINTIES

$$8 \div 2(2+2) = \;?$$

There is a new swear word in America, if not the entire world. It's COVID-19. The virus that has killed more than 150,000 as I write these words is like nothing most of us have ever experienced. It has disrupted our entire economy, shut down American institutions from sports to schools to Disneyworld, and while a vaccine is in the works, continues to be one of the most stunning disruptors to the financial world that anyone has ever seen since the Black Death. When something as unprecedented as the coronavirus hits, many people are tempted to tread water financially.

If you are fortunate enough to stay employed at the same income level as you were before the pandemic, it can be effortless to tell yourself, "I am going to play it close to the vest until this is over.

Just pay my bills and be thankful I still have a job." Others take it in the opposite direction. They think the only way to survive the paralyzation of society occurring all around them is to spend more money to enhance their experiences and feel good about simple things. They will order take-out or go to restaurants more often. They will plan more vacations to safe areas to ease their stress or visit with friends they cannot see as often as they like. They might even be wooed by a massive discount offered on something they want, but do not need, like a new car, and splurge a little extra for the feel-good bonus.

History tells us that chaotic times need not be cause for panic or inaction.

The smart individual who wants to build his or her wealth looks for opportunities in all situations, including times of crisis like financial crashes and pandemics. As Nathan Rothschild put it: "the time to buy is when there's blood in the streets."

If you are a millennial, you might not have been too affected by the bursting of the housing bubble in 2008 and the Great Recession that followed it.

More than likely, your parents are the ones that took the hit, as older Americans saw their 401(k) and IRA retirement plans lose anywhere from 30%-60% as big banks collapsed and the stock market nosedived.

It was a miserable time for most, but plenty of people took advantage of unusual economic conditions to make smart investments that will pan out later. For instance, when the Great Recession hit a little more than a decade ago, an overwhelming number of investors hit the panic button and sold everything they had, fearing they would lose everything. That is a built-in bias that most people have. They are scared of losing what they have. For instance, if you had 500 shares of a stock worth $100/share before the recession, you might sell it at $50/share during the recession because you fear it will drop down to $0 if you want to get something out of it.

The panic of the Great Recession and the ebb and tide of the financial markets of the past few months due to COVID-19 have had a significant influence on millennials like Daisy.

When they read the headlines and see the "talking heads" on the major news channels barking at each other and giving contrary advice, it makes them wonder if investing makes any sense. A survey Capital One Sharebuilder found that an overwhelming 93% of millennials say they distrust the financial markets and are less confident that investing is a good idea. Of that same group of millennials, 40% say cash is the only type of wealth they know.

LESSON LEARNED 15

Just like in a real-life situation, when everyone else is panicking, that is the time for you to stay calm and collected and make smart decisions based on logic instead of your emotions.

Smart investors realize that buying stocks and other financial investments when everyone else is selling them is a bit like grabbing up merchandise from a store during a going-out-of-business sale, except even better. You get items at a fraction of what they are worth, but as a bonus, they are likely to increase in value over time, meaning ultimately, you can sell them for a lot more than you bought them.

History shows that in every global crisis over the past century, from the Germans invading France to terrorist attacks such as those of September 11, 2001, people panic and sell.

The stock market drops way farther than it should, then following an almost immediate recovery, the panicked sellers now have to buy back their old stocks at a much higher price, while smart investors bought low and see an immediate increase in their holdings. You do not have to be a Wall Street insider or a financial guru to do the same thing during times of crisis. What you do need is to learn your history.

Tons of stocks and investments might go through cycles, but they always rebound. For instance, companies that make pharmaceuticals or those that drill for the oil that power our cars are good to research. Precious metals like gold and silver are others that have stood the test of time.

You can also consider what items or commodities people covet during the pandemic, such as rental properties outside of the largest cities. With the metro areas seeing huge waves of infections and more concentrated death rates, not to mention people wanting to work from home more and more, the desire to move somewhere less crowded is top of mind for many Americans.

Learning from the past, both personally and collectively, is a great way to grow and succeed. The coronavirus pandemic is not just an opportunity to profit financially, but to improve on yourself as well. For most people, there is a lot more downtime when most businesses are closed, and many of us work remotely.

Don't just spend it all on social media or binging shows on Netflix. Take some time to delve into your past and see where you have veered left when you should have stayed right.

Pinpoint the opportunities for growth that exist in the wrong choices from your past, and take away the lessons that you can use moving forward towards the goals you have set up for yourself.

The present bestows many opportunities. Most people who are looking to disrupt their lives, hoping to find ingenious ideas do so amid their daily frustrations.

The most disruptive thinker and innovator of Silicon Valley, Jay Samit, urges his followers and all disruptor-wannabes to carry around a notebook. In this notebook, they jot down all the little frustrations they encounter as they go about their day.

Your Homework?

I encourage you to do the same here. In the next few weeks, I urge you to note all the frustrations of your daily routine. Some may be recurring, while others may be new. Either way, I have no doubt some of these frustrations will be the conduit to many uncertainties. Do you want to find the greatest on which to capitalize? Look no further than these notes.

Once you have so dutifully written one-week worth of frustrations, go ahead and review them. Highlight the ones that already have solutions on the market. Cross out those that seem implausible. Put an asterisk next to the ones that have no marketed solutions as of yet.

The next step is to identify which of the asterisked frustrations you wish to dedicate some time to researching, analyzing, and perhaps solving. This exercise might lead you to your first big idea. Go ahead, give it a try, I dare you!

OPPORTUNITIES IN UNCERTAINTIES

CHAPTER 08

WEALTH THROUGH PRODUCTION

I f you are like Daisy, you fancy the occasional retail therapy. And, if you happen to live in New York City, you are no stranger to over-consumption. The idea that New Yorkers consume more than the rest of the country is not an understatement. I have personally witnessed bags upon bags of rubbish tossed every night from the same apartment building. I have even asked once whether there was a factory producing rubbish in said building. My friend kindly assured me that New Yorkers do not like to cook, so they order out or visit restaurants. Whether or not we believe they could eat so much as to produce enough trash comparable to week's amount is a story for another time.

As you probably are, I reckoned that they were also shopping for clothing, household items, gifts, among other things leaving the sidewalks of Manhattan crawling with plastic bags on a nightly basis.

Behavioral economics dictates that they will continue to do so unless the marketers who also happen to live on the island decide to go out of the marketing business. Have you ever heard that "consumption" creates wealth?

Consumption is indeed a precursor to a healthy economy, job development, and expanded opportunities.

However, that consumption must come from somewhere else first. Like the manna that just fell from Heaven, it had to be created. Sure, God may have created the manna, but who created the product or service that we consume today? A tree can only turn into the shelf on the wall above your head through the means of production.

Please repeat after me: wealth creation is a product of production. No, not consumption. If you wake up tomorrow and think to yourself, "I want to buy an egg sandwich for breakfast," that isn't creating wealth. The people creating wealth in this chain of reactions are the farmers who took the time to grow the wheat that became the fluffy bread you are sinking your teeth into before 10 AM.

 Understanding that production is the source of this kind of wealth is the first to change your mind about how to further yourself and your financial independence today.

Just look at China as an example: at least before Covid19, their economy was projected to grow 9% this year. Why? They focus on production primarily, not consumption. They are the worldwide powerhouse provider, and coronavirus has shed light on how dependent we are on this country to create for us.

Therefore, I want you to remember this statement: manufacturing creates wealth by taking resources of lower value, like labor and minerals, to sustain a higher output. There are four sources of wealth throughout the world:

- **Natural resources:** Wars have been fought, blood has been spilled, and alliances are still formed today over the ownership of natural resources. Although this can get political, there are still many resources accessible in any given area of geography. Identifying what is available to you without paying for expensive shipping, etc. is something to consider when building up your production means.

- **Labor:** This commodity increases in value with more education and training. If you put time into investing in your labor, you will control the means of production. Just look at the U.S. manufacturers that survived the 2009 Great Recession. They are now very competitive, working with lower labor costs and debt burdens.

Not to mention, as more people than ever before proclaim, we should take our production capabilities back from China, American manufacturers are being overridden with requests to accommodate new business ideas and shifts. It is known: manufactured goods dominate foreign trade, and U.S. factories are struggling to keep up with demand.

Knowledge: The most important wealth source of all is knowledge. With more knowledge, you can create more productive labor systems and harvest natural resources with greater ease. Through inexpensive and universal communications, knowledge-based work is creating high-quality products and services around the world. If you can produce faster, cheaper, and better, you win!

Entrepreneurship: Recently added to the discussion of production is entrepreneurship, which is accredited with the creation of jobs, the innovation of ideas, and forced waves of change necessary for all industries. Entrepreneurs will take all other production factors to conceptualize, create, and produce the product or service. They bring products to the market at a much faster speed than more giant corporations. The first reason behind this is that they are not bound by endless protocols, office politics, and rigid processes.

The second reason is since they are motivated by an exit strategy that is timebound, entrepreneurs are frequently interested in disrupting as fast and vastly as possible.

Lastly, their agile working models and decision-making allow them the flexibility to fail quickly and still keep up with the changing pace of competition.

How you choose to use and synthesize these sources will impact the kind of wealth you aggregate for yourself. Mining and farming are two classic examples of taking natural resources, like rocks and wheat, and turning them into a product that you may acquire at the store.

Following thousands of mergers and acquisitions, we have normalized the fact that most of our products come from conglomerates.

Unfortunately, another bi-product also emerged: technology started to shift competition: barriers to entry for small producers had become insurmountable. Following the 1990s, however, all that changed. The world's interconnectedness otherwise referred to as globalization, has made it so a young woman could create a hair product from the comfort of her living room. Like her cash-rich competitors, she managed to amass her raw materials, packaging and labeling supplies, and payment processors from her comfortable couch.

Don't allow the negative view of manufacturing related to multinational conglomerates to cloud your view of this wealth-building tool. These companies have no loyalty and will close down plants and outsource without hesitation.

Production is the foundation of economic growth, and on the smallest scale possible – if we're talking about you – it's a great way to accumulate wealth that you own.

As the Greek philosopher, Parmenides, once said, "nothing comes from nothing." One of the best ways to start investing in your financial independence is to create what you sell.

In other words, you must quickly learn to turn yourself from a consumer into a producer. That way, you are not beholden to changes, upsets, or shifts out of your control.

Autonomy is now at your fingertips in this kind of digital world, so what's stopping you? Tell that voice in the back of your head to be quiet. Create, produce, innovate, and breathe life into your ideas, your products. What will you create? The time is now!

USINESS MODEL CANVSA

● Key partners

Who are your most important partners?
Which key resources do you acquire from partners?
Which key activities do your partners perform?

● Key activities

What are the activities you perform every day
to create & deliver your value proposition?

● Value propositions

What is the value you deliver to your customer?
Which of your customer's problems are you helping to solve?
What is the customer need that your value proposition addresses?
What is your promise to your customer?
What are the products and services you create for your customers?

● Customer relationships

What relationship does each customer segment
expect you to establish and maintain?

● Customer segments

For whom are you creating value?
What are the customer segments that
either pay, receive, or decide on your
value proposition?

● Key resources

What are the resources you need to create &
deliver your value proposition?

● Channels

How does your value proposition reach
your customer? Where can your customer
buy or use your products or services?

● Cost structure

What are the important costs you make
to create & delivery your value proposition?

● Revenue streams

How do customers reward you for the value you provide to them?
What are the different revenue models?

CHAPTER 09

WEALTH THROUGH EQUITY

Allow me to start this section on a selfish note. Before you can invest in companies, other people, and ideas, you need to first invest in yourself. There is only one you on the planet, which means at the end of the day. Making time to invest in yourself is the only way to lay a fruitful financial future.

Imagine for a moment that you are the founder of a startup. You are at the point where you want to take your idea or invention to the next level, but you don't have the capital to make it happen. You dress up in a blazer, tie your hair back tightly, and take a big breath before you want into a room filled with investors. They are sitting in their chairs waiting for you, wondering why they should give you THEIR money.

It's up to you to deliver an enthusiastic pitch that sums up all of the reasons why your startup is worthy of investment. You finish the pitch by stating the exact numerical figures you need to meet to move forward. The investors then hit you with a slew of questions. A little sweat pours down your back as you try to keep your breathing regulated while seeming calm, cool, and collected. You find them tricky and somewhat impossible to answer, but you do your best. You're afraid you may need to give over control of your company to win the money you need to push forward.

You walk back into the room, and the investors are ready to tell you their plan. There are one of two things they can do at this point:

- Priced equity round: the investors purchase shares in a startup at a fixed price
- Convertible securities: the investment amount converts into equity

Allowing these investors to have considerable equity at the company works for both parties: the startup is now funded, and the investors are promised a return for their equity investment. Amazon, Facebook, and Google started as startups that needed help to reach their next level.

What makes a startup different from a company, like an airline with physical assets and cash flow to measure, the startup does not have collateral to offer against the loan. So, if the investor wants to feel like the investment is going to pay off, they contribute to buy an actual percentage of the company, known as equity.

In its purest form, equity is the ownership of assets that may have debts or other liabilities. To arrive at the equity figure, you would be required to subtract liabilities from the value of an asset.

So, let's say you just walked back into that room, and the investors tell you they are on board with your proposal, but they want 50% equity for the agreement.

They are essentially telling you they want to control half of the company – with that half, they will have a say in what does and doesn't work. As the company makes more money and progresses, new investors down the line will be willing to pay a larger price per share since the startup has proven it can be successful.

When a venture capital investor puts down capital in exchange for a portion of ownership over the company, they have property and rights to the potential future profits. Should the company make $50 million next year, you'll receive $25 million, and the investors will receive the other $25 million.

How is the percentage of equity ownership calculated? It's the number of shares owned, divided by the total number of outstanding shares.

Who gets to access this kind of investment? Can just anyone invest in a startup? Well, as you can imagine, there's an exclusive community for these kinds of unicorn investments. Startup founders, employees, and investors will all split the shares in a startup. Although the founder starts with 100% in their startup's equity, they will have to give over control if they want to bring on other people.

Investors will decide which companies to invest in if they feel the startup has significant potential and will pay off down the line. That's why your pitch you made in your best blazer is everything.

First impressions are the only impressions in the world of equity trading.

Trap of Entrepreneurship

As humans, we don't like to share. When you were a kid in the sandbox, you didn't want to hand over your toys to other kids. Why? We are inherently selfish and don't want to relinquish anything we feel is OURS. We're afraid we'll never get the toy back, or we won't be able to enjoy our time on the playground like we originally intended to.

That's the problem with equity and entrepreneurship. If you are sitting on a goldmine of a business and have reached a point where you can't take it farther without help, you have to loosen up control and bring other stakeholders into the equation. It is impossible to build massive wealth all by yourself. The most prominent billionaires in the world know if they want to expand their empires, they need to hire people who are smarter than them.

Facebook, Amazon, and Google are in control of the entire world today.

They have grown so significant and influential that the government frequently debates breaking them up. All three of them were born from an equity arrangement. Do you think the monstrosity that is the Facebook empire could have gotten that way without any help?

The entire founding of the platform was created in the middle of in-fighting at Harvard. Everyone wanted in on the action.

Entrepreneurship has a time and a place. It's a great way to explore ideas, go out on your own, experiment, and test the waters. When you finally have something worth growing in the palm of your hands, the consideration of equity becomes essential. It's the only way to increase your wealth beyond the point of your idea and your knowledge.

None of us are superheroes, much to our dismay. We are mere mortals that need capital assistance. Don't be afraid to ask for it.

You have probably heard the saying: "starting a business is the first step in building real wealth." That saying exists for a reason – when you're not paying your future, your labor, and your hours into another company, but rather yourself, you have more control over how much of that wealth remains in your possession.

Of course, this kind of autonomy doesn't come without its costs, like initial risk, increased hours on the job, and the stress of being in charge of an entire business.

If you start a venture now, not just to get supplemental income, but because that's how generational wealth is built, you will unlock a future of wealth you never thought was possible.

If you need some initial convincing, here are a few reasons why starting a business will do more than help you build wealth:

- **Side Income:** Many people today don't rely on just one income for their living expenses. You can run internet businesses while working for someone else. It's supplemental income that can take you from your current income bracket to the next one without giving it "back to the man." Side income will unlock a future of potential that you never thought was possible.

- **Working for Passion:** When you start a business, you get to start a company based on something you love or something that makes you passionate. You're not just going through the motions anymore. Finally, you get to work on something that you love, which will make you work that much harder. With more effort put into the project, you'll witness more return in the form of money.

- **Personal Independence:** As mentioned at the start of this e-book, the American Dream to millennials today is personal independence. It's not about making tons of money; it's about controlling your fleeting time on this planet. By running your own business, you set your hours, but you place your whereabouts. If you start a freelancing business online, you can operate that business from anywhere in the world.

Family Hiring: This is common in many traditional countries around the world – you can hire your family members to work your business to pass on a legacy AND save in taxes. Plus, all money outputted will be going back into your central familial structure, which will help you collectively accumulate wealth more quickly.

Tax Savings: I won't bore you with an entire chapter on the tax savings, but trust me when I say: starting a business is a great way to save on taxes over time. As we have seen, investing your money into accounts that are "rarely taxed" is one of the best ways to build wealth. Therefore, any entity that can help you save on taxes is something you should consider today.

Should You Work for Someone Else

Starting a business isn't for everyone, and for some people, they thoroughly enjoy working for someone else. That's completely ok! If you elect to continue working for someone else, make sure you manage those finances like you would a business.

What does that mean?

It means opting for the rarely taxed retirement plans, volunteer to take on more work and side hustles within the company, invest your time and money into something that will pay off, and work hard to have a stake in the company. You can climb as high as CEO if you put your mind to it. Just look at the example of Carly Fiorina, former CEO of Hewlett Packard. She jumped her way into being the first female CEO in the Top 20 Fortune 500.

Starting a business is neither easy nor haphazard. It will require much work. But the beauty of living in America is that anyone can start a business. With the right amount of planning and preparation, a company can be a great way to expedite your wealth-building to earlier retirement.

Here are some final tips if you are seriously considering starting a business to build your wealth:

- Plan as much as possible. There can never be too much due diligence when it comes to starting a business. Seek out professional support and commentary, and your financial advisor to ensure you set the business up in a way that is beneficial to you and your future wealth.
- Learn every day, all day. If you want your business to be competitive, you will need to know your competition. That means you will need to read up about your industry and trends every single day. Make it part of your daily structure.

- Start small. No one said you need to go out there and launch a large corporation. Start small with a side hustle that you can swell into something bigger. Don't put your life savings into your very first business. Understand that you are going to make mistakes.
- Be patient. Anything worth having takes time and energy. You are going to fail in some capacity. What you learn from those failures will inform the rest of your decisions.

What about Real Estate Equity?

A few months ago, I was vacationing in the City of Gold. Dubai is well known for its motto that can be felt and seen: fastest, biggest, and tallest. They take the same approach to real estate deal-making and investing.

A relatively young woman approaches us at DXB and promises a helicopter ride and view of Dubai from above in exchange for a one-hour presentation about Le Ciel, the tallest hotel in the world.

After much reluctance, we set a date and time to be picked up from our hotel. Admittedly, the visit to Dubai's marina was pleasant and left me asking for more. We also had the rare opportunity to visit the site of the upcoming hotel.

Our guide and account manager then led us back to their global headquarter to discuss the investment opportunity for us as visitors.

She thoroughly explains the benefits of investing in real estate and Dubai. The annual return on our investment would roughly be 7% with a 1% annual appreciation, forecasted on Dubai's October Expo and launch of flying cars, both of which may not occur thanks to COVID19.

I debated adding real estate equity to this section. The reason for that is that under normal circumstances, in my opinion, equity in real estate though it grows does so slowly, too slowly to build massive wealth. For instance, I would have serious issues accepting a 1% growth on any investment. I might as well keep those funds in a high yield savings account. That said, amid uncertainties, this is a hard asset that's worth having.

Daisy once admitted that her ultimate goal is to have a cash flow of $10,000 per month from rental properties. That's a great goal, and there's nothing wrong with it except that she would need to invest approximately $800,000 (that's equity, not market value) of cash to achieve that level of cash flow.

How long do you reckon it would take for someone like our girl Daisy to save $800,000? Years probably, maybe even a lifetime.

And that's the disadvantage with rentals: they don't cash flow enough to generate massive wealth, mostly individually.

While you can buy property at discounted rates, rehab, rent, refinance, and repeat, the path to massive wealth generation will still prove long. The problem remains scalability; you can't scale a rental portfolio the way you could a business. That would require too much capital, too much planning, and overhead, and too much time.

Sure, according to Rich Dad investing in rentals puts you in the correct "Cash Flow Quadrant," but the book does not spell out the amount of time of portfolio-building it would take to create a regular stream of income that ensures the level of wealth we are discussing.

The book also does not mention that you must painfully save to buy one rental property per year, which adds roughly $6,000 to your annual bottom line.

Everyone talks about acquiring rental properties, but no one talks about how darn slow investing in rental properties builds your wealth. Real Estate professionals only talk about how extraordinary rental properties are, mainly because they have a service to sell you and said service requires you to buy real estate.

If you are banking on increasing your net worth by millions in a short time, let me disavow you of this belief. This type of investing is not fast-paced, nor is it speculative. Unfortunately, slow and steady seldom allows you to build massive wealth, though it is the correct attitude to have while investing.

What to Do Instead

If rentals aren't the answer to generating massive wealth, what is?

After discoursing with my wealthiest clients, who own vast rental portfolios, I discerned that none of them made the bulk of their wealth from rental properties. Instead, they opt to invest in rental real estate to diversify their income streams and continue building the wealth they already have at high rates. Investing in rentals came after, or was secondary to, building out a considerable net worth through other means.

They admitted to utilizing the following techniques:

1 They started, ran, and sold a business or multiple businesses.

2 They were in a sales job that allowed them to grow their income quickly.

3 They worked their way into a high-compensation job that always involved stock options.

4 They used their protection planning policies to their advantage.

Investing in rental properties is a great way to build wealth, but as mentioned is nevertheless slow. Instead, start, scale, and sell a business to generate foundational wealth. That business, however, can be real estate-related. Just tap into your current wealth of knowledge and get started.

My wealthiest clients made their wealth through high-income W-2 jobs, sales positions, or owning and selling a business. They then moved that wealth into real estate to create a consistent income stream and enjoy true financial freedom.

Many of these people live within their means and are not necessarily extravagant. You probably wouldn't recognize that they are wealthy if you passed them on the street. But their wealth will outlast them and likely their next generation.

Investing in real estate should be slow and deliberate. It should be a focus but only a supplement to your source of wealth-building. Do not fall into the trap of thinking that investing in rentals will provide you with true financial freedom in a small number of years.

CHAPTER 10

WEALTH IN THE ERA OF THE CROWD

I am on candid camera! That's what I think about every time I think of purchasing a product, and it shows up on my Instagram feed. I don't remember the last time - granted it has been a few blue moons - I bought a hairdryer before checking for an influencer review. Do not judge me; you do that too.

I am a follower. I have been following Patricia Bright for as long as she has been in the business of influencing. I have seen her growth: she has gone from resourceful and cash-poor to innovative and minted. She is the epitome of creativity and brightness. They're out there, these influencers. You cannot throw a rock on social media without hitting a guru, influencer, creator. You might not know their real names, but you have seen their faces, you've seen their channels, you've "followed" them, and you have heard the success stories.

People live beautiful, financially free lives out there who are making the vast majority of their income based on their contributions and personas on social media such as YouTube and Instagram. Does it seem impossible? If it does, it might be because you're viewing how to make money too narrowly. Yes, an overwhelming amount of us makes money by going to a job and working 40+ hours a week in return for a paycheck. That is traditional and safe, and there's nothing wrong with it. But the age of social media and the digital technology revolution has offered up new ways to promote yourself, new ways to connect, and new ways to exchange a brand, voice, and message in return for revenue.

Another excellent example of this is Liz Meghan, who runs a YouTube channel called 'iheartmakeup92'. Since then, Meghan joined YouTube in 2010 and has garnered 707,000 subscribers who have viewed her videos a whopping 28.4 million times! Her channel is dedicated to makeup and fashion, and she reviews products and produces tutorials for women who can buy the products she uses online and follow along with her tutorials on the device of their choice.

As her viewership started to grow, she started getting free samples from name-brand makeup manufacturers to use in her tutorials, giving them instant branding recognition with her followers.

Soon after that, she started getting paid by advertisers to insert their ads at crucial points of her videos. She has hundreds of subscribers now and has made deals with her advertisers that she includes a coupon code for her followers to use if they want to buy the product when she uses their products on her videos. When they use the coupon code, she gets a small percentage of the sale.

Not only is she getting paid to let the companies advertise on her channel, but she is also making money based on someone else's actions, no matter what time of day or part of the world they are in. This is called making passive income, and it is a fantastic way to build wealth: You are making money despite not working. Your previous work and your brand are carrying it forward.

Many people think that Instagram is mostly for posting selfies and taking photos of the delicious meal you're about to eat at a restaurant. Lauren Bath of Australia, a professional chef, found it was the perfect venue to share her two favorite passions: travel and photography.

Way back in 2013, she was a successful chef with close to 200,000 followers on Instagram who loved her delicious dish posting and all of her gorgeous images from vacations. People shared her photos, and a couple of tourism boards took notice, asking her first if they could use her work, then wanting to pay for services, including flying her to their locations and paying for her hotel stay and meals while she photographed her stayed and shared it both with them and the world. When those offers became commonplace, she quit her day job and became what she styles "Australia's first professional Instagrammer."

As we can see from those two examples, making money on social media does not take a master's degree or a one-in-a-million idea. You do not have to be Oprah Winfrey or Bill Gates or Mark Zuckerberg to start making money off social media. Once you find something you are passionate about, you can start making a habit of talking about it, demonstrating it, or showing people how it is done on social media.

Let's get back to our pal Daisy, who grew up on social media like many millennials. She also used to help her mom make wedding cakes and pastries as a teenager and found that she still loves decorating them and doing some baking on the weekends.

It is a great way to de-stress, and they make fantastic gifts for friends, clients, and coworkers. After posting some of her best work on Instagram, Daisy had several friends want to know how she made such great designs without working in a professional kitchen. So she started recording herself doing the baking and decorations and created her own YouTube channel - CrazyDaisyCooks.

She sent the link to friends, and then they shared it with their friends. All of a sudden, she went from 10 views to 100 to 1,000 in a week! People were subscribing and complimenting her and asking for advice on twenty different topics. Even more remarkably, people wanted to pay her to make cakes and cupcakes for their special events. Without even knowing what she was getting into, Daisy had created a side hustle for herself: turning something she loved into a way to open up another stream of revenue.

If you take a good look at yourself, you will find some talent you have that other people do not. Or a passion for something that other people share. Whatever it is, you can find a way to cultivate it into a following social media and potentially a money-making activity. Being passionate about whatever it is may be the most critical thing because it has to be something you enjoy outside of your typical workday.

Daisy loves cooking and sees it as a way to relax after work. If your passion seems like work when you are doing it, it's probably not a passion. When you have your idea that you want to explore, the next big thing is to understand the psychology behind what people respond to on social media.

If you're going to build up a following on social media and ultimately start bringing in revenue from what you're doing, these four essential ideas are necessary.

The first step is to be human. As in let, people see the real you. That is infinitely easier than putting on an act or adopting some crazy personality to draw in attention to yourself.

A great success story from Twitter is a comedian named Justin Halpern. Like plenty of standup comedians, he struggled to get discovered and connect with an audience for a long time. One day he was inspired by something his dad told him to create a Twitter account called "@shitmydadsays," featuring his actual dad's photo as the avatar. He would post a few times a week with lines from actual conversations with his father. It was a huge hit, not just because the lines were funny, but because they were real, and they resonated with pretty much everyone who has a dad. Halpern's account got so famous that it got him a book deal and a TV series.

Once you let people see the real you on social media, you can start building trust. That does not mean a locket with two halves where you each take one part or even a secret handshake. It's more about them seeing you as a consistent source of information that will be real about what you know and what you do not, and give them more content on a pretty regular schedule. That's when it can start feeling a little bit like work – if Daisy posts new recipe videos or baking tips every Wednesday and Saturday, her followers will be expecting one every Wednesday and Saturday unless told otherwise.

If she takes a week off without mentioning it, they will wonder what the heck happened and be upset.

Through trust, you build consistency, and through persistence, you build relationships. When you have a strong following on social media, you'll have relationships with people you have never seen face to face, but who identify you as a friend, a mentor, an older sister, a confidante.

That is a fantastic thing to build because it means trusting you enough to bring you into their inner circle, even if you never actually shake hands or give a hug. When you earn a relationship with someone, it is possible to guide how they buy things and decide how to spend their money.

People are remarkably fickle with their money and whom they choose to give it to. I bet you have a few examples of that in your past.

Want to hear one of mine? I used to live down the road from a beautiful auto repair place with excellent service and a shuttle bus that would take you home and pick you back up when your car was ready. I often gave them my business, but once the lady drove me home after my car got dropped, I started talking about politics in the car, something I do not do with people I don't know. On and on she went blasting a person whom I had voted for. It wore me out. The next time my car needed work, I went to a different repair place because of that bad experience.

The other site was just a different location of the same franchise, but it was 12 miles from my house instead of 1. But that one bad experience sent me driving across town. I did not want to give my money to a person who appreciated my business and did not want to preach politics.

One other part of the psychology of doing things in a public forum we need to talk about. Being online and being seen by dozens, hundreds, thousands, or even millions of people will expose you to the uglier side of the Internet.

There are people out there who will criticize everything you are and everything you say and do, from the way you look, the clothes you wear to every decision you make online. Reading their comments and taking them to the heart can have an unfortunate psychological effect on you; conversely, learning the most positive feedback and believing you are the best thing since sliced bread can have the same effect. Remember that no matter how well or poorly you are being perceived via social media, the most critical version of yourself is living in the real world. Stay grounded there.

When you're getting going on your social media quest, there are a few ways to make money upfront that can help you get some legroom established as your followers grow. You can promote affiliate products in your work, such as becoming an Amazon associate who promotes products you like and earn commissions.

If YouTube is more your game, you can join its Partner Program to make money on advertising that accompanies your videos.

Regardless of what path you choose, the biggest takeaway for you, me, Daisy, and anyone else who has ever wanted to share their ideas with the world via social media is earnest and honest. When you come across as real, you are going to find your niche and your followers.

When that happens, you will start taking on the role of influencer and watch that passion grow.

Your Homework?

The era of influence has proven to be lucrative for some, and I believe it can be for you, provided you have the personality and work ethic required. If you believe this is where you would like to leave your mark, I welcome you to follow the following steps:

- **Select Your Niche**
- **Improve Your Social Media Profiles**
- **Know Your Audience**
- **Create and Post Relevant Content**
- **Be Regular and Consistent**
- **Draw in With Your Audience**
- **Tell Brands You're Open to Collaborations**

Select Your Nice

When you decide to become an influencer, you have to choose your niche. You have to pick a niche that you are keen on and can reliably make content about. Likewise, you ought to have some degree of expertise in the field to have the option to build up yourself as an influencer.

Improve Your Social Media Profiles

When you have identified your specialty, the subsequent stage is to choose your favored social media platforms and make/enhance your profiles. Most influencers are famous on just a couple of platforms. Because of the time constraints, it is best to concentrate your endeavors on only 1-2 channels. When you have chosen your channels, you have to either make new profiles or improve your current ones.

Here are a few things you can do to streamline your profiles:

Change to a Business Account

If you plan on becoming an influencer, you have to change to a business account that opens up significantly more alternatives. Most platforms like Instagram, Twitter, and Facebook can make a business account in the profile settings.

Make an Engaging Bio

Your profile is the main thing somebody sees when they visit your profile and is, along these lines, a significant piece of establishing a special first connection. Your profile ought to have the option to recount your story in a compelling way. Likewise, it ought to give all relevant data about you, such as your complete name, area, contact subtleties, and subject matters.

Include a Profile Pic and Cover Photo

You also need to include a profile picture and a cover image for your profile as they are also significant parts of your image character. Individuals frequently remember an online media profile by the profile picture, so you have to choose an image painstakingly.

Know Your Audience

Before you begin making content and posting via online media, you must understand your intended interest group. Influencers know their crowds and maintain solid relationships with them. That is because of the way that they don't serve everybody. They create content for those with comparable interests in a similar specialty.

Make an Engaging Bio

Your profile is the main thing somebody sees when they visit your profile and is, along these lines, a significant piece of establishing a special first connection.

Your profile ought to have the option to recount your story in a compelling way. Likewise, it ought to give all relevant data about you, such as your complete name, area, contact subtleties, and subject matters.

You should be clear on whom you're focusing on and afterward do it well to attract a dependable following. To understand your crowd, you would first investigate your current follower base to understand your starting point.

Most social media platforms have a built-in analytics tool that provides such insights about your current audience. For example, Twitter Analytics provides insights into your current followers' interests, genders, and locations.

Make and Post Relevant Content

The subsequent stage in turning into an influencer is to post valuable and applicable content for your supporters. The more you can draw in with your crowd, and the more assessments and suggestions will impact the more individuals.

That is the most significant prerequisite for being an influencer, the way that your supporters hear you out.

You have to plan a content technique and utilize a blend of content types, ideally the ones that your crowd will generally like. Some influencers keep their feeds about their picked field of interest like food, travel, style, and excellence.

Such influencers don't blend posts about their own lives with their specialty posts and keep their content concentrated uniquely on their specialty.

This implies a food influencer may post plans, photographs of café visits, audits, and even brand advancements.

Take food influencer Audrey's Instagram feed, for instance. Every last bit of her content spins around food and cafés. She surveys cafés and food brands and posts pictures of dishes that she prefers. She keeps up an assortment regarding the sorts of content but never strays from the cor0e.

Some influencers want to blend in a touch of content from their own lives to better relate to their crowds. Adding presents about their day-on day lives assists influencers with appearing to be more real and relatable. This fortifies their associations with their crowds.

Regardless of what content system you pick, ensure that you make it expansive enough to oblige future brand coordinated efforts. Your supported presents ought to be capable of fit, usually, alongside the remainder of the content you post. You can include surveys as a regular element in your feed, to clear a path for paid promotions that you may get later.

Generally, keep your content concentrated on your specialty, but don't be inflexible. Allow yourself to think outside the box.

Be Regular and Consistent

After choosing the type of content you will post, you have to complete a posting schedule and timetable. Most social media posts' calculations offer inclination to accounts that post regularly. This is particularly true for Instagram, which requires a regular posting schedule to see any real growth.

You can pull off posting a few times per week on social media platforms like Instagram, YouTube, and Facebook. Nonetheless, select the days and times that you will post and be predictable.

An examination by Sprout Social uncovered that there are certain days and times when you can get the most significant engagement on your posts. For most posts, the most elevated engagement rates can be seen during the late morning and evening hours midweek. Wednesday is the greatest day to post for most platforms. You should look at the best occasions to post for your picked platform and construct your posting plan as needed.

Draw in With Your Audience

When you begin posting content via online media, you will frequently get likes and comments on your posts.

An influencer needs to interface with their supporters; hence, you can't disregard these comments.

It is a decent practice to answer to comments and inquiries that your followers pose to you. You can likewise merely "like" their comments to show your appreciation.

Another approach to draw in your crowd is to ask them an inquiry and start discussing a subject of common intrigue. This could cement your situation as an influencer.

Tell Brands You're Open to Collaborations

The last advance towards your journey to being an influencer is to declare it to the world. You have to come out and announce yourself as an influencer who is keen on brand coordinated efforts.

You can do this by writing in your profile that you're an influencer and are keen on coordinated efforts. Likewise, you can give send subtleties to expected customers, giving them a simple method to interface with you.

Another approach to do this is by making your effort and informing influential brands with a pitch on what you can offer. It is ideal to structure an effort format that you can use to connect with various brands, which can spare you a ton of time.

There are a few influencer platforms where brands and influencers can locate one another.

You can likewise utilize those to discover brands in your specialty who are searching for joint efforts.

These are a portion of the more straightforward approaches to search for brand coordinated efforts. A backhanded route is to label brands and notice them when you talk about their items in your posts.

It's essential to make a name for yourself and associate with brands in your specialty. This probably won't yield immediate outcomes, yet will assist you with framing long haul brand affiliations that may prompt future joint efforts.

Recall that it is a cycle that requires some investment and exertion to yield results. Along these lines, you can't hope to turn into an influencer overnight. Be that as it may, if you continue following these tips, you can turn into an influencer and be on your way to creating massive wealth.

CHAPTER 11

UNDERSTANDING THE RELATIONSHIP BETWEEN DEBT AND WEALTH:
USE & DISPOSE

NNot all debt is created equal. While the word "debt" can carry intense anxieties, not all liability is something to shudder at.

I'll admit that the first time I heard about using debt to build wealth, I thought maybe I was still asleep or had not fully woken up yet! I was right out of college, bright-eyed, bushy-tailed, and ready to conquer the real estate world. At seven in the morning, I sat amongst fifteen middle-aged men and women who wanted to learn how to invest in real estate. The well-dressed speaker turned towards us with a giant grin on his face and announced we are half-way through our programming. I am annoyed that so far he had not taught me anything paradigm-shifting. He then quickly transitioned into how to use debt as a way to build wealth for oneself. I immediately perked up in my chair. He finally had my attention.

Debt and wealth were not two terms I was ever previously putting together in my brain unless I was trying to pay down credit card balances and thinking how wealthy Visa and Discover were getting off my debt. Most Americans encounter some debt in their lives.
Millennials know all-too-well the reality of student loan debt, which can seemingly choke their future dreams.

A little debt can be a good thing – but tens of thousands of dollars of debt by the age of 22 isn't exactly your pathway to success.

Can one use debt to build wealth? On the outside, that sounds about as logical as an all ice cream and cake diet to get ready for bikini season, or staying out at the dance club until 3 a.m. to get ready for that big meeting first thing Monday morning. While some of us are fully versed in the different types of debt accounts, most of us are not familiar with the two different debt categories.

Distinguishing between the two categories of debt is a monumental achievement, something our pal Daisy needs to get right with before she digs that credit-card hole any deeper.

Let us roll Daisy's life back to when she was 18 and graduated from high school. She wanted to go to college, but her parents were unable to give her more than a few thousand dollars. She had earned a small scholarship, but all told it would not be suitable for more than a semester, maybe two, even if she worked at the same time, she went to school.

She did not want to settle for just entering the workforce. She wanted the college experience and the increased income potential that comes with it.

Before I go on, please do understand I am not trying to devalue not having a college education. Many people make incredible salaries, attain financial freedom, and are living the American Dream without a formal classical education. Daisy filled out some loan applications and got approved to go to a four-year college to pursue a degree in marketing.

It is no small amount of money, as anyone who has ever taken out an educational loan can attest to it. But doing so is Daisy's look at her first instance of what we call "good" debt.

What makes it good? The fact that you are purchasing something that will likely increase in value over time. The loan looks enormous to 18-year-old Daisy, who has probably never had more than a few hundred dollars to her name. The average total student loan debt in 2019, including accrued interest and the principal, is nearly $33,000.

If Daisy took out the equivalent of $33,000, that is a formidable number to repay when last week you were worried about whose after-prom party to go to and if you wanted your hairstyle for the big dance to be more Ariana Grande or Beyonce. But down the road envisioning how much more money you can make with a college degree than without one, taking on that debt makes some sense.

The jury may still be deliberating on whether it makes sense for education to be this costly or even an 18-year-old must be able to sign for loans of this magnitude. While the opportunity cost, coupled with the amount of debt, make the four-year college experience a questionable one for some, many still consider it one of the least detrimental money decisions people make over the course of their lives.

The same cannot be said for many of her first purchases once she landed that first job out of college. Remember her flashy convertible? It might let all her old friends know how much she has improved her situation when she rolls up in it to visit Mom and Dad for Sunday dinner, but a car fits definitively into the category of bad debt when you are trying to build wealth.

Unless you bought a 1964 Mustang or 1955 Corvette, the wheels you own now are never going to be worth more than the day you bought it. It is a cold, a hard fact of life. Any automobile or any other vehicle – motorcycle, boat, trailer, plane – starts depreciating when you drive it off the lot and begin putting mile 1 on the odometer. If you are going to take out a car loan, the way to do it is to save as much money as you can first for a down payment.

Then use that as leverage to get a lower interest rate or fewer months. Those two factors keep you from overpaying too much beyond the sticker price. This same strategy and definition hold for anything you buy that will lose value over time – otherwise known as suffering from depreciation. Clothes, electronics, and meals are either disposed of or a lot less valuable by the time you get home from the store. They should not cost you more than the price tag on them, but when you go into debt by using a credit card or taking out a loan. Parties and vacations might carry a certain intrinsic value to you, especially if you are a millennial who weighs experiences far beyond material possessions. But from a strictly financial definition, you keep on paying for them repeatedly each month as the interest from the credit card you used to pay for them piles up.

Consequently, Daisy is taking plenty of grief from us for accumulating an exorbitant amount of bad debt in the form of her convertible, her girls' trips, and the splurges she keeps making monthly on clothes or something shiny. Her only good debt to date is her student loan; what else can she do to get back on the good debt side of the equation?

She needs to use her debit card exclusively when she wants to buy something that will depreciate. That means learning how to save money before purchase rather than putting it on a credit card and paying it off later. No more spur-of-the-moment trips out of town on a credit card or birthday blowouts renting a club or a restaurant for the night for her friends. Those things can stay on the social schedule, but they need to be saved up for.

So what kind of good debt can she take on? We know from the last chapter that she has her eye on a side hustle selling cakes and cupcakes for weddings and other social gatherings.

Her kitchen probably has its limitations when it comes to filling big orders or getting things done quickly. If she wants to up her game with the bakery, she can either take out a small business loan or use those credit cards to invest in some better equipment and write it off as a tax deduction next April 15.

Either way, she is using debt to invest in her future with the understanding that taking on debt in the present means increasing the revenue coming into your bank account in the future.

The equipment itself is not going to be worth more five years from now that it is in the present, but what it will allow Daisy to do with her growing home business will allow her to pay it all back and earn a profit beyond the original investment. In essence, she is using someone else's money to give herself the means to build wealth. She will eventually repay the loan plus a degree of interest, but she is using it to acquire skills or equipment that will improve her ability to bring in more revenue.

The ultimate form of good debt, not surprisingly, is real estate. While most people's primary function in buying a home is to give themselves somewhere to live, real estate is best when it functions as an investment. There is a fine line when it comes to investing in real estate, which involves knowing how much house you can afford compared to how much a loan officer says you can afford.

If we learned anything from the Great Recession and the housing bubble bursting in 2008, banks that loan money for homes are more interested in their bottom line than in getting you a house you can afford. Done correctly, however, a loan on home starts building two crucial things: your credit score and your equity in said piece of property.

When Daisy got her first job and first set of paychecks, she decided to splurge on that luxury apartment near the park, her job, and the nightlife center in her city. That is all well and good for her social standing and lack of a commute, but every month she's paying $1,500 of rent money for a place that is in no way, shape, or form hers. It is another excellent look at how financial institutions control people without even knowing it. Renting apartments should be done by people who know they are in a temporary space in their lives, and might need to move at any moment. Renting an apartment and living there for a few years might be convenient and might save you money on things like repairs, but the other end of that cost is staggering.

Like many, Daisy might think that buying a house at a young age does not make much sense. More and more people her age are putting off getting married and starting a family until much later in life, wanting to do their living first – travel, change jobs or careers, really live it up with as few responsibilities as possible.

While readiness level should play a real factor here, why not invest in a condominium, townhome, or an apartment for sale?

Instead, she might find herself paying for amenities similar to a mortgage likely comparable or perhaps even a bit lower than what she is paying in rent. The big difference is that instead of her monthly rent going right into the hands of her landlord, the monthly mortgage payment eventually culminates into equity on the property she owns and another drop in the bucket of maintaining a good credit score. When she does decide to move, that built-up equity, even if it is only a few years' worth, means that much more money she can make off selling it.

We have discussed the strengths of this strategy above, but there are weaknesses to consider as well. Nothing worth doing is without a sense of risk.

Much like any big purchase, the most critical risk to weigh is that external forces might prevent Daisy from paying back her business loan or making her mortgage payments each month. If Daisy worked in an industry that rolled back or furloughed jobs during an event like COVID-19, she would struggle to maintain her ability to pay her bills.

The same thing might happen if she suffered an illness or injury that forced her to take time off work beyond her typical sick leave.

Job circumstances like getting transferred to a new city could see her paying the mortgage on her residence in her old town while also renting or looking to buy one in her new town. There is also always her own family's needs to consider. Remember back at the beginning of this book when we talked about the obstacles and curveballs that life throws at us when we are least expecting them. What if one of Daisy's parents gets sick and can no longer take care of themselves? Daisy might need to use some of her money to help with medical expenses. What if Daisy's sister decides to get out of a messy marriage and needs a place to crash with her children?

There go Daisy's extra free time and money for her baking business. Now she helps prepare meals for four additional people while her new kitchen equipment sits in the corner collecting dust. She will need to be cautious if she wants to risk building wealth through acquiring debt.

A person like our Daisy will have to go about this process slowly and cautiously, but big business people throughout history have used the same method to generate wealth beyond your wildest dreams (not mine though, I have some pretty wild dreams).

One of the people I have always admired is the man whose name is synonymous with family fun, quality entertainment, and some of those memorable movies of Walt Disney. Just think how many characters he drew by hand, created in a movie studio, or continued to appear at his theme parks and movie theaters well past his untimely demise. But the smartest deal Mr. Disney ever produced had to do with real estate. Real estate that not one other single person in the entire United States wanted a single thing to do with. In the 1950s, Mr. Disney opened Disneyland in sunny Southern California, and it was a big hit. But within a decade, he realized that it was landlocked and surrounded by businesses that were not as family-friendly.

Additionally, only 5% of its attendees came from east of the Mississippi River, despite 75% of the country's population living there. Disney started scouting for another location in another sunshine state - Florida - in the early 1960s. He found a spot near Orlando where big highways were aplenty, but literally, nothing else was around, largely because most of the area was a low swamp. In 1964, the Disney movie "Mary Poppins" was a smash hit, recording $31 million at the box office - about $258 million in 2020 currency.

Disney used this windfall to purchase one of the largest land deals in US history.

To keep prices low, Disney formed several dummy companies to buy different land tracts in the same area. If the owner had known that the deep-pocketed Disney was the one gobbling up all those acres, they could have raised the price substantially.

Instead, many non-name corporations were picking up significant tracts of land for as little as $100/acre.

Speculation ran well in the local business community and local newspapers, with guesses on the buyer ranging from NASA to the Rockefeller family to Howard Hughes. It was not until October 1965 that the Orlando Sentinel newspaper "cracked the case" by publishing a rumor that the land grab was for an "East Coast" version of Disneyland. The total property sale covered 25,000 acres. But from the moment the Disney brand was announced, the value of that property increased enormously. Five decades later, it is home to four immense theme parks, 27 resorts hotels, two water parks, a massive shopping complex, and several golf courses.

The power of real estate allowed the Disney corporation to do whatever it wanted to on its new property. The revenue generated from that acreage has been the foundation for some of the most staggering growth. Disney owns the ABC Television network, ESPN, and multiple other entertainment giants, including the Star Wars and Marvel movie franchises.

To consolidate debt, avoid future liability, and better understand your current debt, here are some important distinctions to note:

1 Secured Debt: Secured debt is debt that is backed by an asset for collateral purposes. For example, a credit check is necessary for the lender to judge how responsibility debt has been handled in the past; yet, the asset is pledged to the lender if the borrower does not repay their part of the loan. If the loan is not paid, the asset can be seized. One example of secured debt is a car loan. The lender will provide you with the cash you need to claim the car, but should you fail to pay it off, seize the vehicle from you. Typically, these loans have reasonable interest rates, based on creditworthiness and the value of the collateral.

2 Unsecured Debt: This form of debt lacks collateral. The lender makes a loan based on good faith that the loan will be paid back. If the borrower defaults, they can be taken to court to ensure they give all money owed back to the lender. Some examples of this form of debt include credit cards and medical bills.

3 Revolving Debt: This form of debt is an agreement between a lender and a consumer that enables the consumer to borrow an amount up to the max limit regularly. An example includes a line of credit or a credit card. There is a limit to how much you can spend on each card. Revolving debt can be unsecured, as mentioned above.

Mortgages: Mortgages are the most common and largest debt instruments that most people carry. They are required to purchase a home, with the subject real estate serving as collateral. These loans have the lowest interest rates of any consumer loan product and are often tax-deductible for those who itemize their taxes.

How Do I Determine Good vs. Bad Debt?

There's an easy way to approach debt and classify it generally: does it increase your net worth or have future value? If so, it's good debt. If it doesn't do that and you don't have the cash to pay for it, then it's bad debt.

How Do I Determine if I Have Too Much Debt?

Your debt-to-income ratio is certainly something to monitor on your quest to build wealth. Add up all of your monthly debt payments and divide them by your monthly gross income to arrive at your debt-to-income ratio. Here is an example: if you have a $1,500 monthly mortgage, $200 car payment, and pay $300 for credit card bills, your monthly debt is $2,000. If your gross monthly income is $4,000, it means your ratio is 50%.

Is 50% bad? Generally, yes. It's a rule of thumb to keep your debt-to-income ratio below 43%. Lenders will be less likely to grant you more loans in the future if they see you operate with such a high debt level.

What kind of debts are good debts?

- Taking out a mortgage so you can pay off a house that will increase in value.
- Buying things that save you time and money with a credit card.
- Buying essential items that help you advance your home/business.
- Investing in yourself by taking out student loans for college.

Debt Consolidation

Should you find yourself with five different credit cards that are all carrying debt you can't pay, it's recommended you consolidate your debt onto one credit card. Why? Instead of paying off five different interest rates at once, you can pay off just one simple interest rate. This strategy will help you more strongly manage that debt as you work to build wealth for your future.

Your Homework?

(You get to review your personal debt. Categorise them as good versus bad debt)

CHAPTER 12

BUILD WEALTH THROUGH INSURANCE:
MITIGATE RISKS &
TAX LIABILITIES

We spent our last brunch discussing Junior's overload in energy. At this point, Junior is an eleven-month-old fireball, and he has not the slightest idea of what would happen in a short few months. He had an undeniable bond with this man he would only indeed come to know in pictures. You see, Hector was battling stage three liver cancer. He had been given a year to live. Try as they may, members of his family and close friends were not coping well with the news. I was in complete disbelief of his impending death. I was also optimistic, considering he was being seen and treated by some of the world's best oncologists.

His illness had brought us closer. However, his wife and I shared a real friendship, one that was based on honesty and the sort of trust you cannot buy anywhere. Naturally, I felt her pain, but most importantly, I was concerned for her well being. While she took care of her sick husband and her relatively new baby, who would take care of her? How involved could I get here?

These questions started swimming in my head the day she called to share his diagnosis with me. I ran to Mass General Hospital, fully aware of the gravity of my friend's health. After days of discussion with the oncologists and the family members, a treatment plan was agreed upon. He would start chemotherapy immediately, followed by surgery, provided he was responding well to the course of treatment. Phew, this plan sounds like it might extend his life for a bit. Somehow, we were all a bit relieved to know something could be done, albeit not promising any long-term result.

The planner in me pulled Kate aside. "I understand your pain, and you know I am here with you every step of the way. He's been in chemo and seems to be doing well. Would now be the time to work out a financial plan? Have you thought about that?"

"Nono, she replied. I don't have the capacity yet. This is all too unpredictable right now. We will get it done when things settle down."

The enigma is that everyone needs holistic financial planning, but most are afraid of opening up for reasons that have been well documented. Why did I use the word holistic, and risk sounding like a hipster medicinal doctor, you ask? Financial planning that does not account for protection planning is not considered comprehensive in my trade -- protection planning being at the foundation of the financial house. In Hector's case, there was a severe lack of a plan for life's unpredictability.

We know all too well how unpredictable life can be today. As of right now, over 2 million Americans have contracted the coronavirus. Over 113,000 confirmed deaths have shaken our economies and renewed a sense of "you only live once" mentalities in people. If you had asked anyone in January 2020 about an emerging pandemic that would take hundreds of thousands of lives while forcing businesses to shut down, you would have laughed.

In June 2020, as many files for unemployment and small businesses shut their doors for good, no one is laughing anymore. The need for a "three-month" nest egg was never more apparent than spring 2020.

That's why this chapter holds new meaning. Life happens and presents many risks: divorce happens, grieving happens, and financial burdens, catastrophes, medical expenses.

It can occur when you least expect it. The important thing here is to change your mindset into flexible and adaptable changes to these kinds of changes. Being rigid in your approach to potential setbacks can make them more of a financial catastrophe than they need. I am asking you to accept the unacceptable with an open and realistic mind.

What exactly can you do today to prepare for the unexpected while still staying focused on your financial dream? Here are some ideas.

Diversify Your Portfolio

We mentioned this before, but let us review this idea before we delve deeper into risk mitigation techniques. At its most basic level, diversification is a technique that reduces risk by spreading your money and investments out over different accounts, industries, and categories.

In essence, by dipping your toes into a variety of pools, if one of those pools happens to dry up, your money will be protected in the other resource pools. It only makes sense.

For this chapter, I will discuss the last place you might want to look to diversify your funds.

As mentioned earlier, we all have multiple buckets of money. When people discuss their portfolio, they are often referring to their market-correlated assets such as their mix of stocks, bonds, and mutual funds that may or may not be managed by an investment advisor.

To a holistic financial advisor, however, this is only one (1) bucket of money. While you must ensure that the bucket or portfolio is well-diversified, you must not forget about your other buckets and how they fit into your greater financial plan. Here I am asking you to identify how well all of your buckets are diversified. Do you even have multiple buckets or are counting on only one?

In what follows, we will discuss risk mitigation against market volatility and address mitigating tax risk and circumventing inflationary pressures.

What Happens When You Commit to Diversification?

Mitigated Tax Liability: Taxes play a huge role in how much wealth a person can accumulate over their lifetime. We all have to pay taxes in this country – it's part of what funds a free nation. However, we don't all have to follow the exact tax recommendations for what we are presently doing. Diversification can be an excellent way to diversify your tax liability, so you do not pay as much back to the government every year.

Your accounts will always fall into one of the three following categories:

- **Taxed Always:** these are holdings that require you to pay income tax yearly, like investment brokerage accounts. These accounts may produce interest, dividends, realized capital gains, and capital gains distributions.

- **Deferred Accounts:** The taxed-deferred options are holdings for which you're only required to pay taxes upon withdrawal/distribution. These can include 401(k)s or when any capital gain is realized, like real estate or other hard assets.

- **Taxed Rarely:** these are holdings in which you are rarely (if ever) taxed, like a Roth IRA, interest from municipal bonds, and other kinds of life insurance.

Most Americans will accumulate their wealth through the first two kinds of accounts. The problem with that is that many miss out on opportunities for which they will not be taxed. They don't even realize that there are rarely taxed categories playing a critical role in their tax diversification.

You need to strike a balance if you want to accumulate wealth. It would be best if you went one step further than merely diversifying.

Balances Out Investments

Not all investments are created equal, especially from a tax point of view. Here are just a few reasons why you should pay attention to tax diversification today:

Retirement Income is Still Regular Income:

Everyone knows that contributing to retirement is a smart financial move. What they don't know is that along the way, there is an impact that those 401(k) employer contributions can have on retirement.

Most people assume they will be in a lower tax bracket come retirement.

Every dollar withdrawn from the retirement plan is considered ordinary income, the same as if you were taking it from your monthly paycheck while working.

This retirement fund becomes subject to regular income tax. Those who max out their 401(k) will receive some immediate tax benefit by saving pre-tax, but they may also push themselves into a high tax bracket when it's all said and done. Deferred accounts are still a great option – you want to make sure some of your money is going into the rarely taxed options.

You will spend More in Retirement:

When you are retired, you will have more time. What will you do with that time? Probably buy more things, go shopping, go out to eat, and so forth. Therefore, planning to spend the bare minimum every day in retirement is not a wise move. You should expect a higher cost of living than you are dealing with right now, which is why tax diversification is a great way to ensure this is a reality.

What is the ideal taxation mix for your diversified portfolio moving forward? There is never a one-size-fits-all answer. What you need to prioritize is intelligently accumulating your wealth. Don't be afraid to return to the drawing board, seek professional guidance and support, and change your investments as time moves forward.

Nothing is static in the world of money!

Taxes Are Not Static: Tax planning options change over time. Tax policies vary with presidents and continue to bend and twist to fit the latest political agenda. Based on studies, the top marginal tax rate changes on average every three years, which means your financial situation will change. You will need to adjust this tax diversification plan over time. However, with your side's financial advisor and mostly rarely taxed accounts, you should be able to weather the storm.

The Case for Life Insurance

As CNBC so aptly said in an article two years ago, "most Americans don't know about this one way the rich build wealth." What were they talking about in their provocative title? Life insurance! Precisely, permanent life insurance policies. Contrary to term life insurance policies, which are cheaper, temporary, and come with payouts upon death, permanent policies provide cash-value while still living.

Yes, that means you can enjoy your contribution to life insurance while there is still oxygen in your lungs. You don't have to be six feet under.

When it comes to permanent life insurance, there are a few available policies such as whole life and universal life. The whole life insurance plan is a long-term one with premium payments, death benefits, and other contractual benefits such as dividends. The universal life insurance plan is more flexible while you are still alive. There is also an indexed policy, which enables you to invest in an equity index account.

What do all of these have in common? The accumulation of cash value. If you want to withdraw, you can take out what you have already put in – but you will be taxed. At the time of death, the insurance payout is not taxable, but the cash value can vary depending upon the insurance terms.

Should you put in, say $2,000 per year into an account when your child is born, by the time they are 60, they will have access to hundreds of thousands of TAX-FREE dollars.

Life Insurance helps create a complete financial plan by strengthening the other components. Life insurance offers critical death benefit protection to guarantee a safety net to protect your family, business, and wealth. Permanent life insurance also builds cash value that grows on a tax-deferred basis and, in most cases, can be withdrawn income-tax-free.

Many people don't realize that they could take a loan from the cash value to meet a variety of lifetime goals, such as building a business, providing college funding, supplementing retirement income, or even emergency funds.

Again, the most basic use of life insurance is to benefit your spouse if you are married and your children should anything happen to you. If your family relies on you to be the breadwinner, you must obtain life insurance, often a term policy, as a way to replace your income in the event of your passing.

What should be included in your policy? What is your insurable need? Your insurable need refers to the amount of money your heir would receive upon your death. Most insured families are underinsured because they do not account for all the aspects of your finances that need replacing.

Your insurable need should cover your funeral expenses, account for all outstanding debt, the cost of repaying your mortgage, the cost of education for your child or children, income replacement from your current age to your possible retirement. Thus, insurance can be a genius financial tool that protects continuity and ensures your legacy foundation. Taking out life insurance guarantees your family, partner, or spouse will be able to maintain some semblance of financial stability in the event of your death.

This kind of protection planning is not only mitigation for death. You also have to consider falling gravely ill, but not dying. The majority of people end up losing their entire savings and retirement without any hope of making it back because they did not consider becoming disabled, falling ill, or losing steam. They only think "what if I die prematurely."

While most insurance plans fail to include these, many do provide term policy contracts that allow for living benefits. These benefits can serve you while you are alive, covering the following: critical, chronic, terminal illnesses as well as critical injury. Allow me to break down how each one of these is defined:

- Critical illness include existing and new conditions such as blindness, but are not limited to cancer, ALS, end stage renal failure, heart attack, major organ transplant, stroke, aorta graft surgery, aplastic anemia, cystic fibrosis, heart valve replacement.

- Chronic illness means you are unable to perform two fo six Activities of Daily Living for 90 consecutive days or are experiencing cognitive impairments. Activities of Daily Living include: bathing, continence, dressing, eating, toileting, and transferring.

- Critical injury includes coma, paralysis, trauma, and severe burns.

Look for policies that include these kinds of provisions; some would be in the form of riders, otherwise known as benefits. Not all of them will consist of coverage for critical and chronic illness, which is why I recommend working with a professional when seeking life insurance. To ensure that wealth building is successful, you need to make sure nothing can derail it at the last second.

Plan your legacy through insurance. It's the final piece of the wealth-building pie.

A permanent life insurance policy as an asset class allows you to grow funds in a tax-advantaged account. As a tax mitigation product, you can save for future businesses, supplement your income at retirement, save for educational expenses, and prepare for the rising cost of long-term care.

The funds not used to cover your insurable need, when designed correctly, can grow at least at a 4% rate. When the company declares dividends, as a policy owner, you participate by receiving dividends and the contractual 4% return.

We never want to think about morbid or adverse things happening to us, but we need to be realistic about finances.

Life insurance is also a great way to distribute your assets to partners or spouses and charities, should anything happen to you.

Buy-Sell Agreements through Life Insurance

A buy-sell agreement is a contract funded by the good ole' trusty life insurance policy that can minimize the turmoil caused by sudden departure, disability, or death of a business owner, partner, or someone critical to your business's success. Although we never want to think about our co-founders meeting an untimely death, it's your responsibility to be prepared as a wealth-builder. With a buy-sell agreement, you have one of two options:

- **Cross-purchase plan: This agreement goes into effect when the business owner buys a life insurance policy on each of the other owners. If the owner dies, the remaining owners use the payout from the policy to buy the deceased owner's share of the business. This ensures that ownership of the business remains with the rightful owners at the time of any death.**

- **Entity purchase plan: All owners enter into an agreement with the business to sell their interest in the business. The business then buys life insurance policies on the lives of each owner. Should an owner die, their share of the company passes onto their heirs. The market can use the death benefits to buy the interest from the estate.**

After working your entire life to grow a business into something special, this agreement can ensure that the entity is in good hands.

It can also provide money to create a fair market value exchange, minimize any fighting regarding the transfer of wealth, offer tax advantages, guarantee heirs a buyer for assets, and provide you with some peace of mind – which we all know as an invaluable commodity in the world today.

If you want to mitigate risks and tax liabilities, pursuing insurance as one tool in wealth building is a wise consideration. Not only will it manage wealth transfer, so your spouses, kids, and business owners don't have to, but it will also create a way to accumulate wealth without taxation. If you don't have some of these policies in place, I recommend changing that as soon as possible. Remember, protection planning is at the foundation of any solid financial plan.

Mull Over Other Insurance Options

Don't forget about health insurance, disability insurance, renter's insurance, or home insurance coverage! While you add bills to your monthly budget, these insurance policies will save you significant time in the long run. Please don't gamble living life without health insurance – all it takes is one big accident and one ambulance ride to empty your account of tens of thousands of dollars.

Protect Your Paycheck

Let's pause on life insurance for a moment. Now we're going to look at another insurance option that will help you expand and fortify your wealth.

One of the biggest fears in your life is not being able to pay your mortgage. What if something happens to you and you can no longer work. Or worse, what if you're let go from your job for no other reason than COVID-19 concerns? We are experiencing some of the most unpredictable job market shifts ever right now. One of the easiest ways to cover the loss of earnings is by taking out income protection insurance. How does it work? Income protection pays out a regular tax-free replacement income if you are unable to work because of an illness (coronavirus) or an accident. This payment policy ensures you can pay your mortgage and daily costs of living no matter what.

This kind of insurance pays out a set amount of income after a particular time. You can choose between one and 12-months, with the longer you defer, the cheaper the policy. It will then payout until you elect to return to work, retire, the policy expires, or die (not an ideal option).

Due to COVID-19, insurance carriers are changing some of their policies. Be sure always to check the wording or speak to a knowledgeable agent before you accept a policy you think will be helpful.

Like most insurance policies, the premium is based on age, health, the amount of coverage, the terms of the policy, the waiting period, and whether you smoke (it's time to kick the habit).

For example, let's say you are a 25-year-old adult with a policy that will cover you until the age of 60. The cheapest premium option could start from $9 per month for a four-week deferral period or $6 per month for a 52-week deferral period. The deferral period refers to how long you need to be out of work before you can claim.

Before you elect to take out this kind of protection, be sure to check over your current coverage that may be offered through your job. Some companies are willing to cover costs if you are suffering from an illness or accident. If your company does not, the sooner, the better since this could mean cheaper premium based on your health and age. Be sure to check the portability of the policy, however.

You also want to apply for and accept any coverage before there is anything wrong in your life or with your health – why gamble when you don't have to?

There are always other options, too, as life cover with an excellent critical illness policy that pays out a lump sum should you fall ill. It also tends to be sold with income protection policies.

Disability Insurance replaces lost wages should an accident, sickness, or injury prevent you from working. According to the U.S. Census Bureau, nearly one in five Americans are classified as disabled.

Even if your work provides you with disability protection, it's essential to be aware of the specifics as the benefits may be limited, and the policy might not be portable.

In other words, you may not be covered if you leave that employer.

Prepare for Old Age

Long-Term Care Insurance helps offset the cost of a nursing home or in-home assistance if you become unable to care for yourself. Long-term care insurance can be smart since two-thirds of Americans over age 65 need these services at some point.

When you consider that 21% of people who enter nursing homes need care for five years or more, at an average cost of $80,000 per year, this can financially devastate most families.

Prepare for Natural Disasters

It might seem like recently, more and more natural disasters are happening in this country. Whether you believe it or not, it's wise to prepare for one in the event your home is ruined. These can include tornados, hurricanes, floods, fires, and earthquakes. Many times, like in the instance of Hurricane Harvey, they can come out of the left field and leave you helpless. Consider this kind of expense just if it ever happens, as well as keeping a good emergency kit on your property.

Discuss These Plans with Your Key Stakeholders

Don't keep your spouse or older children out of the conversation. It's best if you tell them about all of these backup financial tools that you have in place, so they know what to do if the time comes. Too many people are afraid to broach the topic, which can leave family members confused and at a disadvantage should anything happen to you. It's also a great idea to bring kids ages 16 and older to your financial advising appointments so they can start learning at a young age about managing their money.

Remember: should you star down any major pivotal life event, please do not attempt to weather the financial storm alone. Financial advisors will be happy to help you make smart decisions when your judgment may be clouded.

Your Homework?

Find an advisor in your area. Inquire about your options for life insurance and disability insurance, if you do not have coverage. Note the answers to the following questions:

What types of life insurance can I choose from?

How much life insurance should I consider? What is my insurable need?

How are the death benefits paid?

Will my premiums change or increase over time?

How can I save money and still get the coverage I want?

For the Over Achievers

You may assume you're adequately protecting what's of value to you. Who will receive your estate? What is your estate currently worth? Do you know what your business interest is worth - has a recent valuation been done? Do you have a Buy-Sell Agreement for your business interests, and is it funded? What are the tax implications for your assets, investments, and business interests? Will you owe federal or state death taxes, and if so, how much might they be? Where will the money come from to pay fees and other settlement costs? Will your heirs have to liquidate your estate to pay the taxes? Creating a financial plan that addresses estate planning and retirement needs can help ensure that you don't outlive assets and enjoy retirement, while still having enough pass on to family and charitable causes.

Your Homework?

Your job is to identify ten estate planning attorneys in your area. Note their names and phone numbers below. Spend 1-hour making calls to determine if they can help you and if you want their help.

EPILOGUE

THE WEALTH BUILDER'S MANIFESTO

 "My interest in life comes from setting myself huge, apparently unachievable challenges and trying to rise above them." Richard Branson

One of my dearest memories is having tea with a successful wealth-builder, Arlene. She is arguably the most intelligent human I have had the good fortune to meet. Arlene told me a poignant surrounding her time working as an agent for Mass Mutual in her early twenties. Arlene, then a bright young woman, noticed that her clients did not realize substantial returns on the funds they placed with her company. She spent months educating herself on the different types of investments. She was searching for a niche where she could provide unsurpassed value.

After months of research, she found herself at the intersection of real estate development projects and deal-making. Ninety percent of the clients she was servicing had decided to join her new practice.

Fast forward to the year 2019, and her firm has structured more than half of the real estate developments in Boston's famous Seaport District.

We all start our lives with big dreams and aspirations. The stories recounted and strategies described in this book are intended to rekindle those child-like dreams and the sense that everything is possible. Your future, your destiny is far more pliable and influenceable than we think. If we take the time to study the systems and financial institutions in which we operate, it is possible to amass massive wealth for our sake and posterity.

No obstacle is so tall that one person with determination cannot conquer.

Every man and woman would like to leave evidence of their existence in the world. This is the wealth-builder's manifesto: to transform your life, your finances, and the world.

According to Forbes, only 13% of the world's billionaires were born into wealth. What these billionaires could probably tell you is that securing massive wealth doesn't just happen. It requires thinking ahead, identifying your needs and goals, and developing a plan to achieve them. Once you have your financial plan in place, it's just as important to monitor it regularly and make adjustments as your life changes and circumstances evolve.

The smartest move you can make is to start planning while you have the time to maximize your savings and earnings potential.

I hope you know that you are worthy of wealth. No matter what anyone has told you throughout your life, you are worthy of a lucrative future that can be unlocked when you seek it out. It takes some people several tries before they are successful in achieving their dreams as they experiment with new ideas and processes. But you do not have to do this alone. I highly recommend you do not do this alone, trying to reinvent the wheel. As aforementioned, every successful person has a team of successful people around them.

In your case, it should be an accountant, a financial advisor, and an estate planning attorney. This trifecta will protect you from all unforeseen hiccups while providing you with essential tools and advice to help your minted dreams become a reality.

Don't hesitate to pay it forward by passing on your new-found wisdom.

Get Minted! is only the beginning of the process of building massive wealth. Get Minted! is a call to action. I hope it has inspired you to transform yourself, your finances, and your world.

ACKNOWLEDGEMENTS

Writing a book is a profoundly humbling experience. While I did not use a ghostwriter or researchers in writing this book, I also did not come to these insights by myself. My approach to wealth building was honed over years of failures and successes. The seeds of my philosophy were planted even earlier, as a young lass, as my dad would entrust me with piles of cash so I could learn about systematic saving.

The insights I've shared in this book are the amalgamation of principles gleaned from wealth builders I have had the pleasure of interacting with and serving over the years. The impact that these encounters have had in my life is immeasurable. I only hope that, in some small manner, this book is a way of paying it forward.

I wish I had the space to thank all who have influenced me. To Sandra Canas, who asked only that I shared my story on wealth management with the then-City Links students: without that one request which led me to speak at their commencement event at Google Inc, I might never have gotten the courage to write about my learnings as a way to teach. To my mother, who taught me the fundamentals of writing: thank you for holding my hand once upon a time so that I can one day hold another's. I owe a tremendous amount of gratitude to Carlos Moniz for walking into my life when you did.

Without you, I would probably be sitting behind a desk and wondering what I had done with the many hours I had been granted.

To Matthew Logan and John Laurito, two of the most empowering and encouraging bosses any financial advisor could ever have hoped to work for: I thank you for having my back and allowing me the latitude to achieve success by breaking the corporate rules again and again.

An immeasurable amount of gratitude to Alistair J. B. Schneider for teaching me about building equity through entrepreneurship. At twenty-two years old, I was thrown into writing a VAE and became engulfed by the idea of building wealth. The caveat was that I had the business know-how to back up my yet-untested ideas.

Special thanks to Ryan Diodato for always keeping me on my toes when my ideas about it would go overboard.

I want to give Ralf S. Rho a big thanks for lighting a fire under me when my fear of releasing a less than perfect (per my standards) book turned me into the procrastinator I warn wealth-builders against. Thank you for keeping me honest and for believing in this project.

I need to thank my friends, who would allow me to test my theories on them.

Thanks to them, you are privy to only information that can be adapted to every situation instead of the reverse.

I am grateful to every elementary school teacher who noted how mathematically inclined I was, and I am thankful to my family for accepting that I would not one day become a medical professional.

I want to thank Ms. Bernadette Desire, a remarkable and intelligent educator who went beyond the scope of work to open my eyes to the world's possibilities. Thank you for always being ready to discuss life's adventures and disadvantages regardless of their magnitude. Thank you for your motherly love.

Lastly, I want to thank people who have mentored me from near and far. I should start with Dr. Sue Davis from Denison University, who provided much-needed support in a tumultuous time in my life, without whom I probably would not have completed my undergraduate studies. Thank you to Cara Drew for being an inspiration to all women in wealth management.

Lastly, thank you to Karen Civil and Patricia Bright, who unknowingly gave me the guts to share my gift with the world. Seeing these women charge forward and be exceptional in their field has inspired nothing less within me.

DEDICATIONS

The dedication of this book goes to the love of my life for inspiring me to look at the bigger picture, see the world for what it is, and find my path to make a difference.

NOTES

Abrams, Samuel (February, 6, 2019) The American Dream Is Alive and Well.
Accessed through:
https://www.aei.org/articles/the-american-dream-is-alive-and-well/
Araujo, Mila et al. July 7, 2020. Transferring Wealth with Life Insurance.
Accessed through:
https://www.thebalance.com/transferring-wealth-with-life-insurance-2645
786
Arth, Larry. May 12, 2018. Building Wealth Through Equity Like The Rich Do.
Accessed through:
https://howtobuyusarealestate.com/the-blog/building-wealth-through-eq
uity-like-the-rich-do#:~:text=Equity%20from%20real%20estate%20has,than%
20any%20other%20income%20stream.&text=As%20you%20trade%20time%2
0for,a%2024%2F7%20income%20generator.
Assadi, Alexis. June 12, 2015. Why Starting a Business is the Best Way to Build
Wealth. Accessed through:
https://www.alexisassadi.net/2015/06/12/why-starting-a-business-is-the-
best-way-to-build-wealth/#:~:text=Building%20wealth%20through%20busin
ess%20ultimately,which%20they%20can%20earn%20incomes.
Buy/Sell Agreements. Accessed through:
https://www.nationwide.com/business/employee-benefits/key-person/bus
iness-succession/buy-sell-agreements/#:~:text=One%20common%20questi
on%20we%20receive,of%20a%20business%20owner%20or
Caldwell, Miriam. August 7, 2019. Tips for Financially Preparing for
Unexpected Events. Accessed through:
https://www.thebalance.com/planning-for-financial-emergencies-2385813
Elkins, Kathleen. December 21, 2016. 11 Simple Money Habits That Will Help
You Build Wealth in 2017. Accessed through:
https://www.cnbc.com/2016/12/21/11-simple-money-habits-that-will-help-
you-build-wealth-in-2017.html

Good Debt vs Bad Debt. Accessed through:

https://www.debt.org/advice/good-vs-bad/

Hamm, Trent. July 22, 2020. How to Calculate Net Worth. Accessed through:

https://www.thesimpledollar.com/financial-wellness/how-to-calculate-you

r-net-worth/#:~:text=In%20a%20nutshell%2C%20your%20net,else%20of%20v

alue%20you%20own.

Khoeler, Mark. Why Starting a Small Business is the First Step in Building

Wealth. Accessed through:

https://markjkohler.com/why-starting-a-small-business-is-the-first-step-in

-building-wealth/v

Ladders. Business News & Career Advice.

https://www.theladders.com/career-advice/8-simple-ways-you-can-beco

me-financially-literate-on-your-own

Lefort, Ben. May 5, 2019. How to Manage Money as a First Generation Wealth

Builder. Accessed through:

https://www.benlefort.com/post/how-to-manage-money-as-a-first-gener

ation-wealth-builder

Pinto, Jim. Accessed through:

http://www.jimpinto.com/writings/creatingwealth.html#:~:text=Manufacturin

g%20creates%20wealth%20by%20taking,wealth%20for%20the%20same%20r

easons.

Rose, Jeff. September 26, 2019. 9 Ways to Build Wealth Fast that Your

Financial Advisor Might Not Tell You. Accessed through:

https://www.forbes.com/sites/jrose/2019/09/26/ways-to-build-wealth-fas

t-that-your-financial-advisor-wont-tell-you/#1ea816d17401

Ruby, Douglas A. 2003. The Creation of Wealth And Economic Growth.

Accessed through: http://www.digitaleconomist.org/wth_4020.html

Simonic, Phil. (September 8, 2017). Tax Diversification: An Untapped Resource

for Wealth Over Your Lifetime. Accessed through:

https://www.kiplinger.com/article/retirement/T055-C032-S014-tax-diversifi

cation-an-untapped-resource-for-wealt.html

Startup Equity Investments. Accessed through:
https://fundersclub.com/learn/guides/understanding-startup-investments/startup-equity-investments/

What is Income Protection. Accessed through:
https://www.confused.com/life-insurance/guides/income-protection
Which Health Insurance Plans are Best for Chronic Conditions. Accessed through:
https://www.hioscar.com/faq/health-insurance-for-chronic-conditions

INDEX

401(k):

This is a profit sharing plan offered through an employer where you set up recurring contributions from your pre-tax income into a retirement account. The employer may "match" contributions up to a certain amount or percentage, meaning they contribute a certain amount for every dollar you put in. Withdrawals from a 401(k)can begin at age 59.5.

501(c)(3):

This is a designation that denotes a nonprofit organization. Companies who offer financial assistance are usually more impartial if they're a 501(c)(3) because their profits are not tied to promoting a single solution that they offer.

529 college savings plan:

This is the most common type of college savings plan parents can use to save up for their children's education. The programs are run by states and educational institutions, but the money saved can usually be used even if your child decides to go out-of-state or to another school. There are usually tax benefits for putting money into this plan.

A

Accountant:

A professional money manager who can help you with all or part of your personal financial management strategy. If you choose to retain an accountant, make sure they are certified (i.e. a Certified Public Accountant or CPA). You can use an accountant to provide assistance in general, or for a specific purpose such as filing your taxes or finding the right debt solution.

Adjustable rate:

This is an interest rate that is not fixed or set at a certain amount. It adjusts at least once or at regular intervals. This means your interest rate may be higher or lower based on certain economic indicators. This is commonly seen with loans, such as an Adjustable-Rate Mortgage (ARM); these loans are often considered riskier than a fixed-rate option.

Annual interest rate:

This is the interest rate applied to your debt over a twelve month period. It may include fees that are applied to your debt or the account. Also called the "annual percentage rate" (APR). The periodic interest rate applied to your balance every month on a credit card can be determined by dividing the APR by twelve.

Appreciation:

The measurable increase in value of an asset over time. Some assets increase in value as time passes, such as fine art or collectibles that gain value as time passes. So an asset can be worth more than it was originally acquired for even if it was purchased at fair market value originally.

Assets:

Any item that has significant cash value to the extent it could be sold for a notable payout or used to settle a debt. This often includes property, vehicles, fine art, collectibles, investments, and jewelry. It doesn't not include things like clothing or everyday household items.

ATM:

Automated Teller Machine. This is a terminal found at financial institutions and other places where you can withdraw physical cash using a debit or credit card. When you make a withdrawal with a debit card, you take money directly from your bank account; a withdrawal with a credit card is called a cash advance. In both cases, you will usually incur fees for using the machine.

B

Bear market:

This is an economic market condition where confidence is low and returns on investments are weak.

Essentially, it's not a good time to invest, but this fear of investment often causes even weaker conditions that cause the bear market to continue.

Bonds:

This is a type of investment where you effectively loan money to a government or other entity at a fixed interest rate for a certain period of time. After that period, the money loan plus the interest earned is repaid. This is a basic type of asset. Bonds can be issued by private companies, states or the federal government, or foreign governments.

Boom economy:

This is a period of time where key economic indicators are positive, which usually inspires consumer and investor confidence. The stock market is stable or growing, consumers are buying, companies are growing, and investors are active. Bust economy: This is a period of time where the economy is considered weak. Investors are not investing, businesses are experiencing slow sales and may face closures, consumers are not spending and often turning to debt to get by. And extended bust is likely to fall into a recession.

Budget:

This is a formalized data-driven overview of income and expenses over a set period of time. A personal monthly budget is usually necessary for a consumer to maintain a stable financial outlook.

A national budget is what the Congress is supposed to set every year that determines how the federal government spends its money.

Bull market:

An economic market condition where stock prices are rising, investment opportunities are strong and key economic indicators are good. This is usually a good time to invest.

C

Cash advance:

This is a physical cash withdrawal made at an ATM or with a lender or checking cashing store. A cash advance from a credit card means you take out money from your available credit line at a high rate of interest. A payday advance is where you borrow money against your expected income based on proof of income provided through paycheck stubs.

Checking account:

This is a standard bank account that you use to deposit money and make withdrawals. The money deposited doesn't earn any interest like you have with a savings account, but you can add and withdraw without penalties using checks or a debit card.

Compound interest:

This is where interest earned over a certain period is rolled in with the principal before the next interest payout is calculated; it's commonly applied to savings and investments. For instance, if you deposit money and it earns a certain amount of interest, that amount is added onto the deposit amount for the next interest assessment.

Cost of living:

This is the total amount of money it takes for you to survive and live comfortably over a set period of time. Monthly cost of living is what it takes for your household to run effectively. If your income does not exceed cost of living, you usually go into debt or face other financial challenges. Average cost of living is something you always want to check before you move to a different location.

Credit:

This can mean several different things in personal finance. Credit is commonly used to refer to money a consumer can access in order to purchase goods and services; it is often paid back over a set period of time. Credit can also refer to an amount of money offered as a discount, such as a tax credit or an account credit where you have a discount on a bill.

Credit card:

This is a financial tool that consumers can get based on their credit rating. A financial institution agrees to extend a certain amount of money to you based on your credit score (or based on a deposit you've made to the institution).

CPA:

The acronym for Certified Public Accountant. Always make sure you're using the services of a CPA if you need some type of accounting service.

D

Debit card:

This is a financial tool tied to your bank account(s) that allow you to withdraw money from an ATM or make purchases using money you've deposited into the account.

Debt:

Money you borrow that gets repaid over time, usually with interest and fees added. Closed-end debt is where you borrow a set amount once and then pay it back over time. Open-ended debt means you have a certain limit based on your credit that you can borrow and pay back cyclically.

Deduction:

Money taken out. Money deducted from your paycheck means you receive a lower payout and instead set aside that income for certain purposes, such as taxes or a retirement account. A tax deduction is money that is taken out of the total amount you owe.

Depreciation:

Decreasing value of an asset over a given time. Some assets lose value – such as most cars. This means you can't sell the asset for as much as you purchased it for originally. If an asset depreciates, it means it's not worth as much as it was previously.

Discretionary expense:

A type of expense that isn't necessary for you to live and doesn't have a set monthly cost. These are the nice-to-have expenses in your budget, such as entertainment and dining out.

Dividends:

The money a company pays out to its shareholders when the company profits. When the company does not profit, dividends may be paid out of a company's reserves.

E

Expenditure:

An amount of money spent for a certain purpose or the act of spending that money. These are the expenses and costs in your budget.

Expense:

This is a cost in your budget. It's money that must be deducted from your income. If your expenses are higher than your income, your budget is out of balance and you're in a period of financial distress.

F

Fair market value:

The amount of money that could be obtained for the sale of an item given current market prices. No matter how much you think something is worth, the fair market value is what everyone else thinks that item is worth – essentially, it's what other consumers would be willing to pay for your item.

File jointly:

This is a filing option for taxes available to married couples. It means that you file your taxes as a single entity rather than as two individuals.

File separately:

This is the filing option married couples choose if they don't want to file jointly. Married filing separately means you each file an individual tax return.

Financial advisor (or adviser):

A professional who assists consumers with understanding their personal finances and making key decisions about their financial futures. An adviser can help you improve your situation or plan for retirement. Always make sure you work with a qualified, licensed and/or certified professional.

Financial power of attorney:

This is the power of attorney you designate to put a certain individual in charge of making key financial decisions for you in case you are incapacitated or unable to make and communicate these decisions for yourself. They handle paying your bills and managing your accounts in your stead.

Fixed expense:

A necessary expense in your budget with a set monthly cost. This are must-pays in your budget that usually have the same cost, such as mortgage or rent payments, auto loan payments, and insurance. These are usually paid first and they're easy to budget for, since you usually know exactly how much money it will cost you.

Flexible expense:

This is a necessary expense in your budget that does not have a set monthly cost. Essentially, it's something you have to have, but you can't plan exactly how much it will cost because the expense varies from month to month. This includes things like groceries, utilities, and gas.

Free cash flow:

The amount of money left over in your budget once all of your bills and other expenses have been taken out of your income. If your monthly household income is $5,000 and your expenses are $4,000, then you have free cash flow of $1,000.

G

Garnishment:

An amount of money taken out of your income in order to satisfy an owed debt. This usually applies to wages or taxes, although garnishment can also happen with government benefits or assistance. A court usually formally determines that a debt is owed and sets garnishments to be taken out of your income based on the total amount owed. Some garnishment such as garnishment for student loans or taxes can be withdrawn without court involvement.

I

Income:

This is money you earn or bring in each month. It includes paychecks, benefits, dividends, government assistance, and court-ordered payouts such as child support or alimony. Your monthly income is the amount of money you have available to spend in your budget.

Inflation:

This is the dollar increase in the price of goods and services that happens over time. It is directly associated with the value of a dollar. When the dollar is weak, inflation occurs more quickly because it costs more to produce goods and services consumers use.

Installments:

This is when a sum money that needs to be paid is divided into equal amounts over a set period of time. If you pay for something in installments, you pay a percentage of the full price spread out over a certain number of payments. With things like retirement benefits, you usually decide if you want to receive a lump-sum all at once or in installments.

Interest rate:

A certain percentage of a debt owed that gets added over a set period of time. The interest rate on a debt means that for each pay cycle that passes, the lender multiplies the remaining balance owed by the rate and adds that to your balance owed. With an investment, the interest rate means your deposit or contributions are multiplied by the rate and your eventual payout increases by that amount.

Investment:

This is any good that is purchased with the intention of earning a profit or getting an eventual payout. This can be a financial entity, such as a stock or bond, or a physical entity such as a piece of property or particular item that you anticipate will gain value over time.

IRA:

Individual Retirement Account. This is an account that you open personally (outside of your employer) for the purpose of preparing for retirement.

With a traditional IRA, you contribute pre-tax income with certain rules and regulations for withdrawal. A Roth IRA is usually more flexible, but the contributions occur after taxes.

J

Joint account:

An account you hold with someone else, usually a spouse. With a joint account you are both liable for whatever occurs. So, if you have a joint credit card that is not paid back, both parties can be pursued by collectors and both people will see their credit scores suffer.

L

Levy:

A fine or fee imposed on your financial accounts due to non-payment of taxes. Essentially, any money put into an account with a levy will be removed for the purpose of settling the debt owed.

Liabilities:

This is basically a fancy name for debts owed. It's essentially the money that you or your estate owes to lenders and creditors, including any remaining balances owed on loans related to asset purchases. Subtracting liabilities from your assets determines your net worth.

Lien:

A legal designation that retains ownership of an asset until a debt is discharged. Basically, if a lien is placed against an asset, you cannot legally sell or get rid of that asset until your debt is paid off. The most common lien issue comes with tax liens placed against your home.

Loan:

A set amount of money borrowed from an individual or company that must be repaid over a certain period of time, usually with interest and fees added.

Lump-sum:

This is a one-time withdrawal or payout of money. Lump-sum debt repayment means you pay everything back at once, rather than in installment payments over a given period of time. Lump-sum withdrawal means you take all of the money available out of an account, such as your 401(k) or a reverse mortgage.

M

Medical power of attorney:

The power of attorney designated to make medical decisions in your place if you are incapacitated or otherwise unable to make or voice those choices on your own. Your designated medical POA decides if medical procedures and surgeries are done if you cannot.

Money market account (MMA):

A specialized type of savings account that usually requires a higher deposit and balance, but also offers a higher interest rate and yield; there may be other restrictions on withdrawals, as well. Also known as a money market deposit account (MMDA) or money market savings account.

Mortgage:

A loan taken out on a piece of property. It allows consumers to purchase property and pay for it over a period of time – usually anywhere from 15 to 30 years. There are a variety of different mortgages available depending on your financial situation and credit.

Mutual fund:

This is a trade-holding investment program funded by shareholders that gets professionally managed by a third-party service provider. When you invest in a 401(k) or IRA, the money you contribute is usually divided between different mutual funds in order to generate returns on your investment. The money given to a mutual fund may be invested in stocks, bonds, MMAs and other securities. If things go wrong or the economy goes bust, the money put into a mutual fund may be lost.

Money management:

The daily oversight of finances. For individuals, this is the day-to-day process of making deposits and payments in order to support yourself and your family. Your ability to manage your money effectively is a key factor in determining your financial success. If you can't manage your account to spend less than you earn, your budget will be out of balance and you will experience financial distress.

N

Net worth:

A measure of your overall financial wealth. It is determined by subtracting your total liabilities (debts) from your total assets. A positive net worth means that you would have assets left over even after all of your debts were paid off in-full. A negative net worth means the value of your assets are not enough to cover your total debt owed.

O

One-off:

An expense that can be planned for your budget because it is not a regularly occurring expense. Things like repairs or holiday expenses are usually considered "one-offs" because they fall outside the boundaries of your regular monthly budget. One-offs usually have to be paid for with free cash flow, savings or by taking on debt.

Online banking:

The ability to manage your financial accounts digitally, either on a computer, smart phone or other mobile device. Also known as mobile banking. In some cases, banks offer accounts designed for online or mobile banking, so you get incentives and/or discounts for doing things like paying bills online.

Overdraft:

When you take money out of an account or make a purchase that you don't have money in the account to cover. An overdraft effectively means you're spending money you don't actually have. This results in cancelled services, bounced checks, penalties and overdraft fees. Some banks offer overdraft protection, which means your purchases are covered up to a certain amount, but additional fees may be assessed.

P

Personal finance:

Everything that relates to your individual financial outlook, including budgeting, savings, debts, investments, and basic money management. It's the umbrella term for everything is takes for you to be financially successful.

Periodic interest rate:

Interest charged over one pay period, as opposed to the annual rate that is charged over a full year. Periodic interest is the rate that gets multiplied by your account balance at the end of a pay period or billing cycle.

That period is determined by you account, but is usually weekly, bi-weekly, monthly or quarterly.

PFM:

Personal Financial Management. This is the name given to online platforms and mobile device apps that allow you to manage your money day-to-day. These tools allow you to manage the money in your accounts with more convenience, such as including all of your accounts in one place or making your accounts more accessible.

Portfolio:

Another name of the sum total of your assets and investments. It's basically an overview of your wealth. A good financial portfolio means you are financially stable with a diversified range of investment accounts and assets that can provide support if you suffer a period of financial distress.

Power of attorney:

The legal designation that makes an assigned individual responsible for making key decisions on your behalf if you are unable to make or voice those decisions yourself. A medical POA makes key medical decisions, while a financial POA controls your money.

R

Recession:

A period of extended economic downturn exemplified with a bust economy, weak consumer confidence, and stagnant business outlooks. In a technical sense a recession happens when a country's gross domestic product (GDP) falls for two consecutive months.

Risk:

This is the potential for a financial investment or action to result in a negative outcome, such as a loss of money or a loss of property. Investments usually come with a certain level of risk, based on how likely or unlikely it is that the money contributed will be paid back with returns or lost completely. Other financial decisions can add risk, such as the added risk of foreclosure that occurs if you take out a second or third mortgage.

Roth IRA:

This is a specialized type of Individual Retirement Account where the taxes are taken out now to avoid taxes later when the money is withdrawn. With a traditional IRA or 401(k) the money you contribute is taken out of your pre-tax income, but when you make withdrawals, you have to pay taxes on the "income" you receive. With a Roth IRA, you contribute money you earn after taxes, but the withdrawals are tax-free.

S

Savings:

Money you have put away for a rainy day. Short-term savings is money you have set aside that grows slowly with low interest added in things like a savings account or MMA. Long-term savings is money you have saved for a future purpose, such as retirement or college savings accounts. This is basically the money you have to depend on in place of income or money borrowed.

Savings account:

A bank account that earns a small rate of interest on any deposits kept in the account. This account is usually used for short-term savings so you have money separate from your basic checking or bank account that's still easily accessible. These accounts should not be your only form of "investment" because they have such a low rate of return.

Securities:

Another name of stocks and bonds collectively. It's a financial tool that has cash value and counts as an asset. Securities are issued by companies or governments to individuals who purchase them with the intent to make a profit as a shareholder or bondholder.

Stock market:

A stock exchange where shares of companies are bought and sold by individuals and investment firms.

Stock:

The money a business raises by selling its shares. Essentially, ownership of a company is divided into bits (shares) that are sold as a commodity or asset. These shares are purchased and when the company's "stock" goes up, the shareholders receive a portion of the profits, paid out as dividends.

T

Treasury note:

A security issued by the federal government (U.S Treasury) that has a cash value with a fixed interest rate and set period to reach maturity. In a really basic sense, it's a personal loan you give to the federal government, who then has to pay you back after a certain amount of time with interest added. Also called a T-note.

Tax return:

This is the official filing you have to make to the government that declares how much you've earned over the past year and how much you must pay in taxes, determined by calculating your income minus deductions and credits.

Federal income tax returns must be filed on April 15 every year for the previous year, unless an extension is filed.

Tax refund:

A sum of money that the government gives you back for an overpayment of taxes.

In most cases, whether you're a W-2 employee or employed individually, you give a certain amount of money to the government at regular intervals (i.e. every paycheck for W-2 employees); if it's determined when you file your tax return that you overpaid, you get money back. A large tax refund isn't doing you any favors; you should decrease your withdrawals if you're a W-2 employee and get a huge refund every year.

Trust:

An account where you can put money in for another individual, usually with certain rules that govern the withdrawal. Money put into a trust is no longer yours by law; as a result, your lenders can't go after the money in a trust in order to settle your debts. Trusts are often set up for children as part of the inheritance of an estate.

U

Utility:

This is a basic public service you pay for the privilege of using. It includes things like water, electricity, gas, sewage and garbage services, telephone, and Internet. You pay for these services every month to avoid stoppages in your service. These are typically flexible expenses in your budget, because the amount you pay each month often varies.

W

Wealth:

This is the sum total of your personal finances. The cash you have plus savings and investments and assets, minus your debts and other obligations. Wealth is formally measured using net worth.

Wealth manager:

This is another name for an investment manager. It's a qualified professional who helps you decide how to invest your money and whether or not you're ready to make key purchases. If you are uncertain about investing, it's better to hire a professional like this than to avoid investing at all.

Will:

A formal document that defines how you wish for your estate to be divided in the event of your death. Your will must be signed and dated and witnessed by at least two other people who also sign as witnesses; public notary can also help avoid problems with inheritance and division of assets. You can designate certain assets and items to go to certain individuals or entities such as business or charities.

Y

Yield:

This is the money you earn from the accrued interest on an investment. The expected yield on a particular investment is another name for the expected rate of return, and it can help you determine if that investment is worth your money.

CPSIA information can be obtained
at www.ICGtesting.com
Printed in the USA
BVHW060859261221
624838BV00016B/2017